MANUEL ARTURO ABREU

INCALCULABLE LOSS

D

INCA Press

TABLE OF CONTENTS

7
NOTES ON THE GARAGE RESIDENCY

21
IS THEORIZING CANNIBALISM ETHICAL?

47
RHIZOME ARTIST PROFILE:
MANUEL ARTURO ABREU

63
GAMING THE SYSTEM:
MONGREL'S "BLACKLASH" AGAINST
STEREOTYPES IN 1990s VIDEOGAMES

81
THINK DIFFERENT:
MONGREL'S "HERITAGE GOLD" AND THE
COMMODIFICATION OF IDENTITY

95
AGAINST THE SUPREMACY
OF THOUGHT

125
ONLINE IMAGINED BLACK ENGLISH

161
TRANSTRENDER: A MEDITATION ON
GENDER AS A RACIAL CONSTRUCT

191
IS THE FACE A SCREEN?

207
INCALCULABLE LOSS

NOTES ON THE GARAGE RESIDENCY

I grew up in the Bronx, undocumented. Now I make ephemeral work in Portland using what is at hand, which mostly goes undocumented.

To clean up its image as a druggy egghead haven in the wake of two fatal student overdoses, Reed College arrested me and my roommate on campus the day before Valentine's Day, 2012. It was touted as a successful drug dealer bust. We were both evicted from campus housing. He was expelled; I was suspended for a year. I experienced a period of housing instability, eventually moving into a detached garage in back of a punk house called "The Blue Velvet," where Reed students formerly lived. After about a year and a half of living there, I decided to call my inhabitation an artist residency. I still live and work here today.

**The Blue Velvet House in Southeast Portland.
Photo via Google Maps.**

While my parents primarily just type URLs into their Google search bar, I knew that at any moment their digital literacy could increase and lead them to search for me. I didn't want them seeing results pointing to my arrest and subsequent court-ordered outpatient rehabilitation, so I decided to brand myself as a poet and artist in order to manipulate the search results for my name. I started a new Facebook account, began submitting work to wherever, and put in my year of sobriety in order for my felony charges to be dismissed (I got lucky). My output had slowed dramatically since high school, but I felt I could still identify and live as a poet-artist despite barely making work.

Outpatient rehab graduation keychain.

What began as concealment of crime via SEO became a sincere fascination with ephemera, disappearance, and what it means to be "performative." I can tell it is sincere because when aesthetic work amounts to nothing is when I feel the most grateful: daily jogs with my mom for a month last time I was home in the Bronx, an abandoned flurry of emails, a one-day installation of found objects and detritus in a recently-vacated room, a failed attempt to change this house's name from "The Blue Velvet" to "The Rossellini." Documentation can always be manufactured, but for me, nothing beats the specific joy of a work disappearing forever, sweetly, remaining only when invoked in language.

The garage between the Blue Velvet.

This fascination developed in tandem with the precarity of my income and housing, to the extent that I sometimes saw the odd jobs and freelance gigs I cobbled together for survival as a facet of my practice, since they also sometimes altered the search engine results for my name. I finished rehab and returned to Reed to graduate in 2014 in linguistics, but couldn't find work until January 2016. My income oscillated between $4,000-$8,000 a year, and I worked variously as a janitor, social media marketer, SEO copywriter, small press managing editor, data entry drone, research assistant, and transcriptionist. Scarcity seemed to engender a slippage between inhabiting a space and making a work in a way that was easier for me to embody than to explain. Treating wage work as aesthetic practice was a lazy way of answering the question: if "there is no art without laziness" (Stilinović), how could I be an artist when poverty is so expensive and labor-intensive?[1] I couldn't afford to be lazy, to sit around and think and write and walk without worry. I needed to eat.

---

1. Mladen Stilinović, "In Praise of Laziness," Atlas of Transformation, originally published 1993.

It's worth pushing back against the idealization of laziness. From Aristotle to Paul Lafargue, many praises of idleness situate work as a demeaning activity reserved for the unfree. Lafargue says "the Greeks in their era of greatness had only contempt for work: their slaves alone were permitted to labor: the free man knew only exercises for the body and mind."[2] As a person who comes from slaves, I can't abide this kind of framework, not least because it erases the reality of slaves across history using slow labor, bad labor, refusal of labor, and other similar tactics of laziness as resistance to their masters, but also because it flattens slavery and its afterlife simply to "forced work," when this is only one aspect of its infinite violence. This formulation of laziness doesn't offer any useful critique against the idea of work, it just condemns slaves and workers.

manuel arturo abreu, *untitled*, 2016; stone, dirt, grass, moss.
For snap (Compliance Division, May 2016).

---

2. Paul Lafargue, *The Right to be Lazy* (Oakland: AK Press, 1883).

This is simply a transposition of the worship of work made possible by secularization. As a de-Christianized colonial institution, Western art, like capitalism and socialism, treats work as salvation, whereas it was formerly a curse: "For even when we were with you, we gave you this rule: 'The one who is unwilling to work shall not eat'" (2 Thessalonians 3:10, NIV). Secularization released work from its association as punishment for "original sin," allowing capitalists and communists alike to reconfigure it as a blessing, a right, a path for redemption from starvation and squalor, a way to become human. Treating laziness as salvation, as "the mother of perfection" (Stilinović) is only an inversion of this framework (whoever is not lazy is not an artist).[3] Analogously: when a person becomes legible as an artist, and when an object, process, or idea becomes legible as art, from what are they being saved?

Discourses of work and laziness both often rely on the same underlying concept: dehumanization. Whether one takes the capitalist/socialist position where work is humanizing, or the anti-work position where laziness is humanizing, the contrast is clear—one wants to be human, not inhuman. Since settler colonialism positions Black people outside the human category, the discourse of labor "does not explain Black presence, Black labor or Black use in white settler nation-states" (Tiffany Lethabo King). King opts instead for a framework of fungibility to analyze the ways the settler state uses Blackness to meet "desires beyond those of labor and profit."[4]

---

[3]. Mladen Stilinović, "In Praise of Laziness," Atlas of Transformation, originally published 1993.
[4]. Tiffany Lethabo, "Labor's Aphasia: Toward Antiblackness as Constitutive to Settler Colonialism," *Decolonization* (June 10, 2014).

Just as the labor analytic is inadequate for explaining the role the Middle Passage and its afterlife play in capitalism's development, so too is a laziness or non-work analytic. And the deficiencies of such humanizing discourses carry over to the aesthetic realm, not only falling short in the context of explaining Black art, but also manifesting as tokenized inclusion which reifies white settler institutions. Humanist assimilation plays a concealing role, the same way the concept of the wage conceals the violent, fundamental devaluation of the unwaged activity on which it relies. Brooklyn artist Winslow Laroche has a great term for the position of rejecting such frameworks: the "postartist."

At least since Hegel, the idea of the "end of art" has served to critique the development of aesthetics, as well as the relation between making and thinking. For Hegel, the West is "beyond the stage at which art is the supreme mode of our knowledge of the Absolute," because art's dependence on the sensuous caused it to fall behind thought.[5] In a similar vein, Allan Kaprow deployed the term "postart" to describe conceptual and post-conceptual work which, in ostensible contrast to modernist aesthetics of high art as "ritual escape from culture," blurred the line between banal life and high art.[6] For Kaprow, "nonart is more art than Art art."[7] This seems true, given the far higher aesthetic potential of that which is not art in comparison to that which has been "trapped" in/as art, unable to return to the mundane or the theoretical, frozen and hoarded like a bauble in a mausoleum. But

---

[5]. Hegel, Georg Friedrich Wilhelm, *Hegel's Aesthetics: Lectures on Fine Arts*, trans. T. M. Knox (Oxford: The Clarendon Press, 1975).
[6]. Allan Kaprow, "The Education of the Un-Artist, Part I" (1971), from *The Blurring of Art and Life* (Berkeley, University of California Press: 2003).
[7]. Ibid.

this blurred boundary easily accommodates market logic, and is itself dependent on a labor/laziness analytic.[8]

manuel arturo abreu, *untitled*, 2016;
dirt, plastic, black watermelon seeds, dried eggshell powder.
Photo by Forrest Wilson.

As opposed to Hegel and Kaprow, a Larochean postart concept is inflected by the Middle Passage and its afterlife, allowing it to question the valorization of objects that exist in a purgatory between commoditized art and nugatory nonart—precisely the fungible position the slave occupies under white supremacy when passing through the *longue durée* and violent value circulation toward false citizenship. Instead, by dismantling the typical work and anti-work discourses on which analyses, tokenizing in-

---

8. Donald Kuspit's old-fogey critique of commercialized postart, *The End of Art* (Cambridge: Cambridge University Press, 2005), makes this quite clear, despite treating the criticized work as a stand-in for the market itself.

clusions, and dismissals of Black aesthetics often rely, Laroche's postart allows us to argue that far from living in a time "after art," the West has not yet actually reached the conditions for art: all the West knows as "art" since the Enlightenment is an ecology of criteria for inclusion which relies on the colonial subsumption of Black and Brown aesthetics. The conditions for art as a fundamentally non-functional or non-utilitarian endeavor will never emerge as long as art's erasure of its own debt to Black and Brown practice continues. The descendants of the Middle Passage have long known that all sociality and aesthetic practice is always-already subsumed into the commodity form under capitalism, since this is precisely what was done to our ancestors, and continues today in the prison industrial complex, where slavery is legal as punishment for crime.

These days, weed is legal in Oregon, and as of June 2016 I work full time as an IT Compliance Analyst/Office Assistant. I recently contributed work to a group show at Reed College for their annual Arts Week—like nothing happened. As I acclimate to my first real moment of financial stability, I can't help but bemusedly wonder: if my life is, for now, no longer precarious, what does that mean for my art? From a postartistic perspective, all it does is allow me to buy materials for once, and more fully understand that I may just not have "a practice" the way people usually mean. Stability doesn't necessarily require a shift away from ephemeral gestures, but few will deny that ephemerality gains artistic cachet primarily in relation to two crutches: true/imagined marginality, and overexplanation. Both sidestep the fundamentally middle-class anxiety that the image of the waged artist evokes, in a marketized landscape where it is both necessary and anathema. Let's end on a third sidestep: frankly, I'm happy just sharing my money with family and friends.

manuel arturo abreu, *untitled*, 2016;
dried chaga mushrooms, wood, dried eggshell powder.
Photo by Forrest Wilson.

IS THEORIZING CANNIBALISM ETHICAL?

"The Indians aboard call this Bohio and say it is very large and has people there with one eye in the forehead, as well as others they call cannibals, of whom they show great fear. When they saw I was taking that course, they were too afraid to talk. They say that the cannibals eat people and are well armed."
 —Columbus, November 23, 1492

"...if said Cannibals continue to resist and do not wish to admit and receive to their lands the Captains and men who may be on such voyages by my orders, nor to hear them in order to be taught our Sacred Catholic Faith and to be in my service and obedience, they may be captured and taken to these my Kingdoms and Domains and to other parts and places and be sold."
 —Queen Isabella, October 1503

1.
SEEKING A TYPOLOGY OF CANNIBALISM

The desire to theorize cannibalism from a non-cannibalistic cultural framework is inseparable from the disgust cannibalism arouses in the theorist. I am not disgusted by people-eating, and thus I am not interested in theorizing cannibalism *as such*, but instead in thinking about *how* non-cannibalistic cultures deploy the trope of "the cannibal," and to what ends. I seek to consider whether the following premise has any merit: theorizing cannibalism is unethical, in that it is an exclusionary maneuver for determining *how human* certain kinds of people are and thus how they can be treated. This is done by means of a conceptual slippage between the categories "human," "cannibal," and "animal." In considering whether theorizing cannibalism from a non-cannibalistic cultural framework presupposes—and thus confirms—

the taboo on cannibalism in the West, I ultimately aim to show that "cannibal" is a non-objective category (Arens 1979).

It's important to distinguish degrees of *incorporation*. This is important because the Western revulsion toward cannibalism only manifests itself at more extreme ends on the incorporation continuum. Consider the following points along this continuum: nailbiting; Pliny's vampirism (he maintained that drinking blood cured epilepsy); post-natal placenta consumption. While blood play is still seen as "deep kink," all three of these examples presumably would not invoke the same repugnance in a cannibalophobe as would cases of lethal cannibalism. And a pathologized instance of lethal cannibalism, such as the case of Armin Miewes, would presumably incite more revulsion than the Donner Party, since the latter was a "dire case," in which ethical axioms are temporarily "tossed aside."

Even the cannibalophobe is willing to admit that in dire situations, lethal cannibalism is "unavoidable" for the West. It becomes clear in such situations that "when people have to eat people, they do," so to speak. But then why does the West avoid this practice when it is not absolutely necessary? Is there anything deeper than a basic revulsion to people-eating, or is that it? Is it some sort of parametric epistemological difference between cannibalistic and non-cannibalistic cultures such that for the former, the parameter is "off"— whether defective (corrupted) or undeveloped (primitive)—and people-eating is not repulsive? If so, then it could be maintained that for certain people the category "human" is defined as "that which is not to be eaten." However, a structuralist approach of this kind seems ill-fated, given that the parametric theory cannot capture potential culturally-cannibalistic practices where revulsion toward people-eating is in fact at play. It presupposes, in other words, that disgust and desire are mutually exclusive.

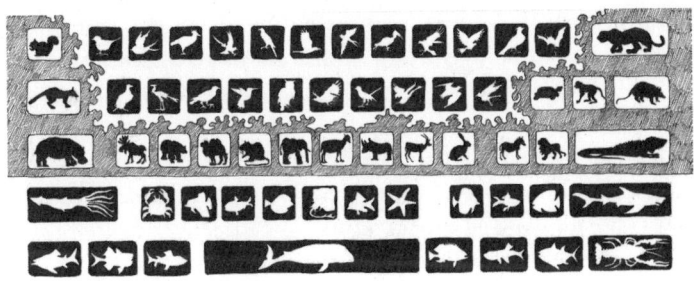

Illustration by Antonia Stringer.

Either way, variation of this nature motivates me to seek a basic "typology" of cannibalism, so to speak: what factors are at play in a given instance of people-eating, whether "cultural" or "pathological?" First, cannibalism either does or does not happen as a culturally-acceptable practice (acceptability can be gradient cross-culturally). This is clear from the stigmatization of the Miewes case: it is because lethal cannibalism is not acceptable in the West that a trial against Miewes was mounted, even though his victim gave full consent. Second, cannibalistic practices can take exo- or endo- form: exocannibalism is when people eat people from outside their communities of practice, while exocannibalism is when in-group members eat each other. Thus, eating one's dead ancestors as an act of worship or love would be endocannibalism, while eating one's slain enemies (whether as an honorific or desecrating ritual) would be exocannibalism. Third, cannibalism can be literal people-eating or it can be metaphorical, as in colonization.

Just as degrees of incorporation apply for "literal" cannibalism, they also apply to "symbolic" cannibalism. What is the latter? A simple example would be the Eucharist. Consider another example: Arens (1979) mounts a critique against the foundation of anthropology, positing that early accounts of cannibalism by Western anthropologists had no factual basis, and only served to justify the West's own "cannibalistic" imperial tendencies. Of course, in laying the groundwork of such a claim, Arens (as I posit is inevitable in theorizing cannibalism) nevertheless evaluates cannibalism negatively: white colonization was bad because it savagely cannibalized other cultures by characterizing *those* cultures as savage cannibals even as there was no evidence. A similar line of argument might apply to globalization. But despite Arens' unquestionable good intentions, his analysis leaves us were we started: people-eating is repulsive, and one should not lie about whether another is cannibal in order to exploit that other (Columbus never met any cannibals, though he wrote in his 1492 journals that New World natives spoke of such practices on other islands, and thought initially that the Christians were cannibals; by 1494, Columbus was claiming that "as amongst all these islands, those inhabited by the cannibals are the largest and the most populous").

Even in such a seemingly-radical proposal, the theory still has not left the realm of the normative: the negativity of cannibalism is presupposed. Moreover, since cannibalistic practices *are* in fact attested, Arens' theory seems even less feasible.

The equation "eating human flesh is dehumanizing" dehumanizes those cultures where cannibalism occurs. But further, the idea that the West and anthropology are "bad for being cannibals" can itself then only be a projection of the misshapen idea that cannibalism is bad to begin with: this kind of analysis crumbles from its own assumptions, since as Arens himself posits, "cannibal" as an anthropological category is a non-objective *a priori* component of our definition of the human. If it is possible to exit the normative circle that structures discourses on cannibalism in advance, and thereby to apprehend the phenomenon "neutrally," it will require radical conceptual-terminological analysis.

2.
THE PLAY OF DISTANCES

The original andropophagi were noted by Herodotus as a nomadic, lawless tribe of people-eaters near Scythia. The more familiar term *cannibal* comes from *caniba*, Columbus' rendition of the Carib people's emic name—as well, it was reported that they, the *caníbales*, ate human flesh, and the meaning of the word as we know it arose. As well, I note that the origin of "Caliban," as in Shakespeare's *The Tempest*, is from a version of *caníbal* with the "n" and "l" interchanged, attested in Hakluyt's *Voyages* (1599). What is the relationship between the cannibal and the Caliban, besides being near-anagrams in Spanish?

As the etymology of the word attests, Arens is not totally incorrect. Western cultures have long condemned far peoples as people-eaters to justify the way the West treated them, and Queen Isabella's decree quoted above shows that the labeling of New World natives as "cannibals" directly enabled their enslavement. But Arens's misstep is in assigning badness to cannibalism *per se*. Badness belongs to the *theory* of the cannibal, so to speak, not the cannibal himself. Or, more precisely, the badness of cannibalism consists in the conceptual linking of "cannibal" with "inhuman." After all, the introduction of "cannibal"—there is no theory of X, no science or -logy, without terminology—served three semantic purposes: to name a people, to name a practice, and to ineluctably link the two. Joined with the underlying assumption of revulsion toward people-eating, *naming* the Caribs as such was clearly politically effective: these were inhuman practices, and those who practice them deserved to be treated inhumanly.

What is it that allows the linking of people-eating and inhumanity? Diderot begins his *Supplement to the Voyage of Bougainville... on the Inconvenience of Attaching Moral Ideas to certain Physical Actions which they do not Presuppose* (1772) with a conversation between two philosophers. B asks what will happen when a given island's populace begins to multiply and resources dwindle. A responds that, obviously, cannibalism will emerge, until some means of procuring other resources arises. On this argument, then, Western civilization is precisely this means: it renders "cruel" practices like cannibalism, which were essentially means of controlling population growth, unnecessary, and thus repulsive (this is questionable since cannibalism as population-control can lead to species death). Athenagoras' line of argument, however, sees the revulsion toward cannibalism more as a maxim than as a result: on his account, if people do not adopt the maxim that cannibalism is repulsive, civilization falls apart—they begin eating each other and doing "however many other things nature allows." On this view, cannibalism is not an anomalous state that occurs outside (prior to) the condition of civilization. Rather, cannibalism is a bottomless hunger that must be restrained if *philia* toward the social body is to be maintained.

In light of these examples, I hypothesize that cannibalism and inhumanity are linked because of the Western notion of the *sacrality of the rational body*. The self-conscious being, with future plans and goals, is thwarted in these interests when she is killed: her higher-order thought dissipates into "mere flesh," as it were, and following Athenagoras, if humans become food, then all order is lost. Thus, a cultural system which practices cannibalism is, on these accounts, "cruel" and "ancient" in origin, as well as "lacking" in *philia*. Simply put, the cannibal as cultural category is inhuman for the West because it denies precisely that most basic tenet of being human: as Harman put it, being "that which is not to be eaten."

What is yonder is labeled not human, and this is the play of distances with respect to theorizing cannibalism. What is yonder is animal, or anthropophagic. It is notable that far-away, non-urban communities may not share the urban architecture of separation from other animals in the biotic community. That is, the development of the "city" primarily served as a means of removing animals, aside from the "domesticated" ones, from the daily experience of Western citizens, except when presented as food. The geographic distance between the urban and the animal leads me to consider the conceptual distance between urbanity (the concept of the city or *polis*, the site of the political and home of the "political animal") and animality.

In this context, it is interesting to note that Marx excluded animals from the proletariat. Marx entertained an essentially Cartesian model of animal experience (unfeeling organic machinery), even while acknowledging that animals are capable of labor. The difference between, say, a beehive and a building is that a human has an idea in her head of the latter, while bees have no idea of the former (Capital, Vol. I, 283). In this way Marx reflects much of the literature on animal ethics: some relevant trait differentiates humans from non-humans, rendering the former (and, for some theories, not the latter) actual laborers / moral agents. We can see how this ties into Western notions of the cannibal as inhuman and thus more animal-like.

For much philosophy, the establishment of "universal categories" is seen as more powerful than the attention to difference. But there can be no establishment without some kind of motivational state seeking to create hierarchy. This is at the essence of Harman's critique of Peter Singer: if an ethical framework like Singer's posits that we should treat animals equally, it would logically follow that eating humans is as ethical as eating animals.

But since built into the very concept of "human" (and therefore Singer's argument for animal liberation) is the notion that a "human" is a "thing of a kind which is not to be eaten as food," there is a disanalogy between humans and animals, at least when it comes to what can be considered for food.

The concepts of "cannibal" and "animal" are thus inextricably related through economic categories of production and consumption: animals were phased out of daily urban life and the entrenchment of factory farming began. The "cannibal" as category arose historically from European imperialism, and following Arens' proposal that "cannibal" is a non-objective category, I posit that it is by naming certain humans "cannibalistic" and thus "less human" that the treatment of those thus named is normalized.

3.
WHAT DO ANIMALS ACT LIKE & WHAT IS ETHICS?

The child learns to eat the meat on her plate but is scolded for harassing the pet. She learns early on, then, that "animal" can occupy a state which is either less human (and thus available for violent acts such as eating) or more human (and thus to be respected as autonomous agent, and not, say, have its tail pulled). Depending on the context, the child may early or later on learn that humans, too, can occupy these different states: televised wars make it clear that it is *okay* to kill certain humans abroad *for reasons*, but that certain other humans are not to be killed.

Just as pets can both occupy and not occupy the category "animal," and just as slaves were both non-human property and clearly human (since the master does not eat his slave), the anthropological "cannibal" can be posited as a non-human human, which can be seen in a 1525 image in which canine snouts identify New World cannibals as non-human (Klarer 391):

The common-sense notion of ethics in light of the slippage of categories like "human," "animal," and "cannibal" is thus as follows: we treat "people" like "people" and "animals" like "animals" because *people do not act like animals*, and we treat humans that do act like animals as they appear to be. We learn how these (sub)categories act based on the representations to which we are exposed. The initial steps toward a solution to this untenable philosophical situation, then, consist of pointing out the incommensurability of different epistemic modalities across human-constructed categories, as well as the fundamental violence involved in positing non-human animals and certain kinds of humans as locations of comparison, as sites of articulation.

One might argue that an entity is a moral agent if that entity is able to play the ethical language game. Because animals do not communicate using human language, they aren't able to "play" the ethics game. *Prima facie* there already seems to be a problem with this language game: we are determining how to treat a set of beings without allowing them access to the language game on their own terms. This is not a language game at all, since all of its affected parties have not agreed to the rules (see Wittgenstein's *On Certainty*).

The crucial facet of the language game of ethics is that *the players decide what to do*. Characterizing animal ethics as "how we should treat animals" presupposes and reifies the power relation that a true animal ethics should seek to challenge. What I argue here is that every object of inquiry has an ontology which emerges as a response to the violence of inquiry, and that a language game which calls itself "ethics," that is, "the search for a good life," should be rigorous with respect to its meta-language, since as Harman shows with Singer, an argument can proceed without making certain assumptions clear, and this is a sign that we should tread carefully. (My only operative assumption is that it is *good* to be explicit about one's philosophical assumptions).

Let's consider this "ethics language game" notion further: ethics looks like a performance dictating normative action. It is inscribed by law, in the sense that an ethical injunction becomes much more powerful when law is involved: I kill the mosquito that bites me and not the human that bites me primarily because the latter action, while satisfying whatever motivational state caused it, would result in the bigger harm for me. Law serves as the "ground" of ethics in this sense. We know this to be true because the idea of killing a person is contextually different from the actual action.

In the case of the utterance or the idea, tone and context matter heavily. Consider the difference between a lover saying teasingly to another "I'll kill you if you eat the last piece of pie" and a lover saying the same thing with a knife to the other's throat. Let's say this situation's two variants are video-recorded, because of the house's security system. If the addressee dies a year later and police can get a warrant to find the tapes in the house, it would be much harder to mount a legal case of intent to kill against the living lover if the only evidence was the video of the teasing utterance, as opposed to the video of the knife assault. However, if along with the video tape of the teasing utterance a notebook describing ways of killing the lover is found, then a much stronger case can be made about intention.

I take such a circuitous example because I follow a Wittgensteinian approach to ethics, motivational states, and interiority: there is no private language, and therefore no private mental states. Instead, there exist partly-nonlinguistic, physiological motivational states which confer sensory stimuli with impetus: it is these motivational states which are responsible for the fight-or-flight response, as well as for the rhizomatic mutability of human affect and epistemology, given language's recursivity. Sensory stimuli do not of *themselves* cause us to act, or to think; they interact with the organic machinery in such a way as to *produce* what is ready at hand. The role of ethics for this kind of argument is thus sentimentalist and epistemic: it is a method of discovering *how to treat* the Other.

4.
MISREADING ARMENTROUT FOR "GOOD"

By "sentimentalist" I mean that the ethical framework I am positing here does not assert the objective existence of ethical value "out there" in the world: instead, ethics is about feeling. Value is asserted in a heuristic fashion.

A misreading of section 1 of a poem called "Yonder" by Rae Armantrout provides a useful illustration:

> Anything cancels
> everything out.
>
> If each point
> is a singularity,
>
> thrusting all else
> aside for good,
> "good" takes the form

> of a throng
> of empty chairs.
>
> Or it's ants
> swarming a bone.

In the case of ethics, we can misread "for good" here and read into Armantrout a sentimentalist viewpoint: for her, ethics are a feeling, articulated at a point in time. If ethics is "everything about how to be good," then "anything cancels / everything out." The second and third stanzas suggest that the point of ethical articulation, as a singularity, only considers the good. "For good" retains its idiomatic meaning, while the ethical singularity-point thrusts "all else / aside" irrevocably ("for good") as it seeks the form of the good.

Each of the two last stanzas offers a metaphor for the form of the good—that is to say, for the form not only of what is sought, but also of what is thrust aside, canceled out by any given singularity-point. Given the disjunct, Armantrout's singularity-point leads to a binary-branching structure: the form of the good is *either* the "throng / of empty chairs" *or* "it's ants / swarming a bone." Thus, if we take each point of experience and ethical articulation to be an instance of the "anything" in stanza 1, which can cancel everything out "for good" by virtue of its search for "the good," then the ethical and the irrevocable take the form of one of these two elements. I believe Armantrout offers the disjunct in these last two stanzas as a way of exploiting the ambiguity of "for good," and it is this ambiguity which affords my reading here.

Is that which is thrust "aside for good" the set of empty chairs or the ants swarming a bone? The same question applies for the ethical. Can they both be both at the same time, or switch between them depending on context? Following Armantrout, if *each* point leads the irrevocable and the ethical to take one of these two forms, then it is *at each point* that "good" takes one of these two forms. It is this mutability that leads "anything" to cancel everything out.

This mutability is inherent to the language game of ethics: the motivational states underlying the language game are the theory-external machinery which render it functional. My misreading emerges more clearly, then: in the performance of the ethics language game, anything—any kind of motivational state—can cancel out "everything," that is, the entire ethical theory. Ethics is not only a sentimentalist domain dictated by the singularity of each point of articulation/experience, it is also not an empirical domain: the form the "good" takes is a cryptic, elliptical disjunct. Further, the poem suggests it is not the ethicist who decides upon the form of "good," only that "good" *takes* form.

The two images Armantrout offers for the form stand in stark contrast. The first is a set of human-designed functional objects, unused. Use is implied but the image is static, and the production process remains concealed. The second image is of a process: a system of organic beings extracting use from a bone. But the source of the bone is concealed, just as the source of the chairs. In the latter case we presume a human source. Both images hold tension with respect to concealment and explicitness, as well as proximity and distance thereof—and we note the title of the poem, "Yonder."

It is tautological at best to ask, in the context of Armantrout's post-L=A=N=G=U=A=G=E idiom, "what these images mean." It would be better, instead, to mobilize my misreading for the topic at hand. How can these two forms that "good" might take with respect to a sentimentalist ethical framework help us understand the slippage between categories like "human," "cannibal," and "animal?"

The chair image posits ethics as design: intentional, rational, functional. But note that the chairs are empty: ethics is not being *used* in this case of anything canceling everything out. Instead, "good" simply takes the form of this "design" of ethics which is invoked in the performance as a kind of formal gesture (and thus "empty" as the chairs are). My claim here is that every theory of cannibalism which posits cannibalism's inherent badness is of the "empty chair" kind: it simply invokes an arbitrary schema or design to justify its underlying assumptions—whether they be that taking human life is bad, or that humans are not to be eaten, or that cultures are not to be appropriated.

Which brings me to the ant image. Here ethics is articulated as in organic motion or flux, not necessarily intentional, and relational in a way that seems quite different from the aesthetic relationality of the designed empty chairs. The ants do not necessarily *relate* to the bone in the same way that the chairs relate to their designers: the ants are simply *acting* on the bone. Ethics here can even be seen as instinctual, depending on one's "theory of ants." As well, function is not really in question with respect to the chairs: they are for sitting in, and they are unused. But what are the ants doing with the bone?

Presumably they are extracting use-value from the bone. Positing the ethical—that is, performing the language game of ethics—is thus a similar kind of value-extraction, a swarming. But we keep in mind that the images form a disjunction: the "good" takes the form *either* of empty-chair ethics *or* of swarming-ant ethics. This is not to say that use-value is not extracted in the empty-chair case, only that the form "good" takes is different when the ethical language game is performed. Use-value is extracted by empty design or by ineluctable swarming.

Therefore, with respect to the question of whether theorizing about cannibalism from a non-cannibalistic perspective is ethical, Armantrout offers two potential, cryptic answers. In the course of my misreading, I have only discussed "empty-chair" theories of cannibalism. This kind of use-value extractions can be seen in Harman's claim that "human" is "that which is not to be eaten," thus rendering all those who do eat human flesh "inhuman." This description, not coincidentally, applies to both non-human animal predators and human cannibals. Again: what is yonder is posited as inhuman: as animal or anthropophagic.

When we ask "what is good?" and more specifically, when I ask "is theorizing cannibalism good," "good" takes one of these two forms, metaphorically speaking. What does this mean for my purposes?

5.
WHAT WOULD A SWARMING-ANT THEORY OF CANNABALISM LOOK LIKE?

Non-cannibals since Herodotus have been fixated with this non-objective category (see Avramescu's *An Intellectual History of Cannibalism*). Asking whether cannibalism is good or bad characterizes the cannibal as an *other*. This is why I am positing that theorizing cannibalism is unethical: the very terms of inquiry marginalize the supposed "matter at hand." Theorizing cannibalism doesn't contribute to understanding the cannibal, but rather mobilizes a certain ethical design, "a throng / of empty chairs" meant for rational beings whom are not to be eaten: whether those beings are Athenagoras *philias*-full non-cannibal citizens, or Arens' culturally-marginalized ostensible benefactors, or the vegetarian moralist's humanized animals. All of these ethical designs perpetuate the fiction of the rational ethical agent.

But is theorizing cannibalism always bad? What would a swarming-ant theory of cannibalism look like?

Theorizing cannibalism as "good" or "bad" tends to entail objectionable conclusions. So far I have only mentioned theories which evaluate cannibalism as negative—theories that can be boiled down to the maxim "people, whatever they are, should not be eaten," applied to different domains. Instead of positing that this theorizing is *good*—since this puts the theorist in a tough spot, having to argue, for example, that colonization, from which the word, and thus the theory, originated, is "good"—I want to try to circumvent the entire argument: if we consider the question of whether theorizing cannibalism is ethically *necessary or unnecessary*, instead of *good or bad*, more interesting results emerge. This question stems from a resonance in Armantrout's empty-chair and swarming-ant images: the chairs are necessarily relational to their human designers, while the relationality of the ants and the bone is not a necessary one.

An answer in the affirmative is tempting in light of two potential advantages. For one, it would bind us to the duty to understand cannibalistic cultures. For another, it would compel the theorist to adopt a conceptual-terminological analytic method—to delve into the tangle of terms to come away with a more verisimilitudinous representation of the "facts at hand."

The latter advantage is somewhat sneaky, since the theorist's new method is meta-theoretical (what is being theorized is not the cannibal itself but rather theories of cannibalism and their entailments).

This puts the theorist in a double-bind, and "cannibalism itself" is never reached: instead, aspects of the theory are posited as "cannibalistic," as Arens did with respect to anthropology, or as Derrida did in his interview "Eating Well," where he posited that the calculating/rational subject is constructed through the cannibalistic sacrifice of the non-subject.

But what of the negative answer—the claim that such theorizing is ethically unnecessary? This claim seems actually preferable to me. If the theoretical enterprise that seeks to determine the nature of the cannibal is fundamentally complicit with the enterprise of colonization, then no methodical supplement will suffice to exonerate the anthropo-phago-logical inquiry of its ethical badness.

It seems to me that the question *Is theorizing cannibalism ethical?* is analogous to the question *How similar is this instance of cannibalism to the Eucharist?*

The Eucharist is an instance of symbolic cannibalism. The bread and wine in the ritual are the flesh and blood of Christ, in consubstantiation. It is in the prevalence of this ritual in Western thought and practice that the questions of the ethics of cannibalism, as well as the ethics of theorizing cannibalism, gain cogency. It's easy to imagine missionaries of yesteryear in far-off places coercing "cannibals" to take communion—to eat the body of their Savior instead of the bodies of their enemies. As well, on a kind of Freudian analysis, it becomes clear what the underlying mission of theorizing cannibalism actually is: to sublimate actual flesh-eating to the rarefied realm of theory, to the Eucharist dimension. Of course theorizing cannibalism could be argued to be ethically necessary, but only if the underlying assumption of such a proposition is the inherently ethical nature of the Eucharist.

A swarming-ant meta-theory of cannibalism would argue, then, that theorizing cannibalism serves as a kind of conceptual imposition of the Eucharist upon other cultures, which echoes missionary and colonizer logic. Indeed, the theorizing of cannibalism perpetrates the illusion of its own necessity, which follows from the importance of the Eucharist in Western culture. Eucharistic notions seem prevalent to me in idioms like "food for thought," in which what is inquired is consumed, and Derrida's argument with respect to subjecthood as a "necessary" cannibalism can be seen in this light as similarly Eucharistic, since for him we always-already cannibalize the Other to construct the terms of subjecthood.

Even as Derrida's argument can be attacked on these grounds, he makes an important point regarding the role of the play of distance between "human" and "animal" in constructing the myth of the rational agent: humans can be fucked but not eaten, while animals may be eaten but not fucked. Implicit in this normative Western dichotomy is a claim about animal rationality which deserves unpacking. It is because animals cannot consent that we do not fuck them—they do not play that language game. But of course, if they cannot consent to sex then they also cannot consent to being eaten. The solution to this lies in Marx's notion of the animal as unfeeling organic machine without relations: animals" inability to consent reveals that they are not rational—they have motivational states, but no sense of *who* is experiencing them, no continued sense of self over time, etc. Since animals are not rational, *unlike* humans, they are okay to eat. And likewise, those humans who historically have been deemed irrational were "kosher" in a symbolic sense.

This gets at the essence of my claim: that "human" and "animal" are categories of reproductive capitalism. These categories are no less objective than is the category "cannibal." They serve to perpetuate the myth of the rational, calculating subject, the arbiter of the binary (yes/no, either/or, good/bad, real/unreal). The significance of my claim that theorizing cannibalism is unethical is that any attempt at interrogating such behavior (literal or symbolic) with a binary-ethical language game betrays the heteronomy of the motivational states underlying ethical maxims. Derrida fails on this reading because if subjecthood is always-already cannibalistic and the Other can never be fully subjectivized, then the question becomes how to "eat well" (*bien manger*), which succumbs again to binary-branching.

6.
THE HYPOCRISY OF THEORIZING CANNABALISM

The Eucharist is one manifestation of Western cannibalism. Around the same time that New World ostensible-people-eaters were called barbaric, Europe trafficked heavily in medicinal people-eating, as attested by Samuel Johnson in his dictionary of English (1785). Consider the following recipe by Oswald Croll (ca. 1560-1608, translated and quoted in Noble 2003):

> Take the flesh, unspotted cadaver of a redheaded man (because in them the blood is thinner and the flesh hence more excellent) aged about twenty-four, who has been executed and died a violent death. Let the corpse lie one day and night in the sun and moon—but the weather must be good. Cut the flesh in pieces and sprinkle it myrrh and just a little aloe. Then soak it in spirits of wine for several days, hang it up for 6 or 10 hours, soak it again in spirits of wine, then let the pieces dry in dry air in a shady spot. Thus they will be similar to smoked meat, and will not stink.

Paracelsus argued that violent deaths trapped the souls in the bodies, and that these were the most prized comestibles. I mostly quote Croll's recipe in perverse delight at the prose, but Croll and Samuel Johnson show that cannibalism in Europe was not only common and seen as medicinal (this derived from the third-century philosopher Galen), but also elaborate. Clearly Europe is hypocritical, then, in condemning so-called "cannibals" in the New World while practicing literal people-eating and attesting a long history of medicinal incorporation (recall again Pliny's maxim that drinking blood cured epilepsy). And of course, the Eucharist and medicinal cannibalism are a case of the-chicken-and-the-egg. Whence the difference with respect to New World and medicinal cannibalism, for Europeans? An answer to this might lie in a decree in 1604 by King James I, according to which only those skilled practitioners licensed at the Barber-Surgeon's company were allowed to dissect human bodies. Naturally, this decree prevented citizens from freely engaging in body-dissection, and medicinal cannibalism became a matter of the law. The New World cannibals, then, might have been called barbaric simply because they were not "eating well," not eating meat medicinally—the structure of their cannibalism did not *resemble* that of European cannibalism, whose logic is Eucharistic and was became professionalized after James" decree.

Indeed, it was only by distancing their own practices from those of the New World that Europeans were able to maintain the (positive) medicinal value of their flesh-eating. European medicinal flesh-eating was positioned as rational, human. This can be seen in the *London Pharmacopoeia* (1618), which included entries for mummy, human blood, and human skull. New World flesh-eating, on the other hand, was *indicative* of the perceived animality of those people. With this in mind we can update both Derrida and Arens: it is not that subjecthood is always-already cannibalistic, but that Europe was *literally* eating people, and needed to distinguish their people-eating from the people-eating of the people they conquered. It is not merely that "cannibal" as Western category is non-objective, since it condemns in others what Europeans do. It is in fact an *erasure*, a way of ignoring the actual European practices in order to use the category metonymically in the animalization of other humans. For lack of a better analytic tool, I invoked the Eucharist to make my point clear: theorizing cannibalism is the question of asking *How alike is this to the Eucharist?* This does not only a priori establish the Eucharist as inherently good ("Jesus said unto them, Verily, verily, I say unto you, Except ye eat the flesh of the Son of man, and drink his blood, ye have no life in you," John 6:53), it establishes the medicinal status (that is, the Eu-charism) of European flesh-eating.

The *theorizing of cannibalism* itself is a kind of meta-theoretic performance positing its own necessity, because the theory itself reifies the (shaky) premise of the inherently ethical nature of the Eucharist. Theorizing cannibalism sublimates non-European cannibalism to "the Eucharist dimension," so to speak, for it is only in this "metaphysical" colonization that questions relating to the ethics of cannibalism (i.e., non-European people-eating practices), or the ethics of theorizing cannibalism, can be asked. In this way, theorizing cannibalism, whether it is ethical or not, is hypocritical.

RHIZOME ARTIST PROFILE: MANUEL ARTURO ABREU
By Eleanor Ford

The latest in a series of interviews with artists who have a significant body of work that makes use of or responds to network culture and digital technologies.

Eleanor Ford:
You describe your book *List of Consonants* (Bottlecap Press, 2015) as an ambient novella, built from text you self-plagiarized from your writing following your friend's suicide, entries on social media/online forums, and what you've called "real" found texts. Did you see this process of mangling of your past-works, or perhaps past-selves, as a means of creating a new corpus that resembles a hypertextual exchange? Or, alternately, does it reform

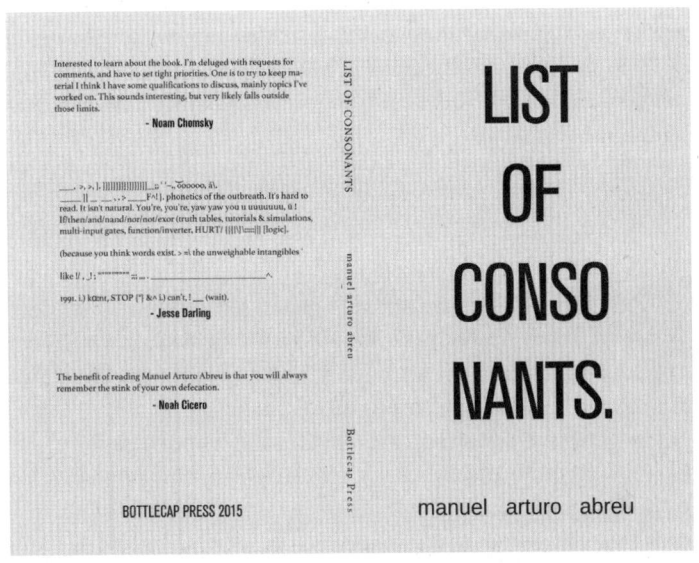

manuel arturo abreu, *List of Consonants* (Bottlecap Press, 2015).

texts preserved and found on the internet towards an organic, perhaps more human, structure?

Manuel Arturo Abreu:
After my friend passed I wrote tens of thousands of words in mourning—very purple prose, selfish centering of my own feelings, mostly unusable. It felt good to write daily, so long and much, from scratch (for the past few years I've generally worked with found text). As such, I felt I needed to use that text somehow, maybe "sculpturally." In the act of merging this from-scratch text with various kinds of found text, I was thinking about recycling, the commodification of trauma, and Wilson Harris's notion of community-in-creator, which posits the self as a debt to the contexts and communities from which it emerges: "my voice" isn't really my voice, it's an assemblage, both vessel and vector for violence. I did partly feel a slippage between mourning my friend and trying to talk to him. I was also thinking of the peculiar guilt of losing someone and having it become a reason to keep going, but also a reason to talk over him, or through him, which seems bad, but necessary.

I wanted the text to complicate the commemorative, which is seen as the payment of respects but in fact incurs more debt to the dead, debt which is ultimately unpayable. I saw the process of forging the text as managerial: I generated the bulk of it in one sitting of about 60 hours. I wanted to set a trap for myself, not only through asking what the difference between from-scratch and found text is, but through the challenge of authentically performing the resulting texts (such as at poetry readings). In destabilizing the authoriality and authority of "my voice," I tried to find a middle ground between the L=A=N=G=U=A=G=E dictum that confessionalism, indeed narrativity in general, is trite/apolitical, and the feminist dictum that the personal is political.

EF:
The internet as a source for research came to a head in your online performance *Servicio Digital a Papá Legba* (2015), where your own "noob aesthetics" in the practice of Dominican Vudú were put on display to an online audience. Does this kind of provisional religious practice, in comparison to an individual raised in generational contact with the traditions of Vudú, perform a circum-generational reclamation of heritage? A neo-theological interpretation of the Vudú traditions that have made it onto the internet? Something else?

MAA:
The trope of the researcher coming to gradually embody the object of analysis is so cheesy that I may regret divulging this, but my neophyte religious activity stemmed from research into an Afro-Cuban syncretic religion's social media presence, which I presented at ACLA 2015. Its name was homophonous with an Afro-Dominican religious musical genre, which was my jumpoff. I am less interested in reclamation or authenticity, and more in the way that, as an Americanized immigrant, my relationship to island Dominican (vs. diasporic Dominican) cultures is heavily mediated, apart from my family, through consumer commodities, be it the internet, the people I talk to on it, or the content I engage on it.

I find myself with one foot in both the "displaced person" and "privileged Westerner" categories. The former denies me access to my provenance, while the latter affords me a certain level of protection. This renders my religion both provisional and provincial, but I think people come to their faiths in many ways, and the digital can act as a platform to encounter severed lineages and parallel timelines. As a performance, the piece was pretty much just me praying the way I would if I weren't being recorded. However, as a simultaneous target of and vector for violence, I feel that making public my somewhat-makeshift beliefs was a way of engaging these issues: Does the mediated nature of my relationship to Dahomeyan-Haitian deities weaken my ability to petition them? Conversely, what role does the institutional platform play with respect to this mediation? I was also thinking about Sheilaism.

EF:
You and Victoria Anne Reis (a BHQFU alum) started home school this year, a free pop-up art school in Portland that acts against the current MFA-obsessed culture of arts academe. Can you talk about the aims for the project long term, your personal experience teaching and how you're deciding on instructors?

MAA:
home school honors the etymology of "school," from the Greek *skholē*, meaning leisure, rest, free time. I am interested in casual rigor, vernacular pedagogy, and the relationship between marginality and institutionality. Our curriculum consists of classes, talks, exhibitions, poetry readings, and more. We are currently in pop-up mode to investigate the relation between site and discursive texture, as well as to challenge ourselves in navigating Portland's ephemeral project space scene, which, despite (or because of) its parochialism and precarity, enjoys a degree of regional and sometimes intra-national clout, even canonicity (Appendix Project Space and its aftermath is a good example). But we do hope to find a home at some point!

Victoria and I chose participants mostly nepotistically: my e-friends are pretty amazing. The first semester of 2016, which began in March, features two classes (one taught by me and one by Victoria), as well as remote talks by Hamishi Farah, Eunsong

Eunsong Kim at Duplex for home school, Portland, OR, April 24, 2016.

Kim (pictured here), Rosemary Kirton, Jesse Darling, and Jamondria Harris. The second semester features a class taught by you (Eleanor Ford), and a class taught by Portland performance troupe Physical Education (keyon gaskin, Allie Hankins, Lucy Lee Yim and Takahiro Yamamoto). We'll also feature talks by Devin Kenny, damali ayo, Gaby Cepeda, Sonia Choi, Winslow Laroche, Sasha Puchalski, and Taj Bourgeois. I'm so excited!

EF:
Shifting gears a bit: a marketized art education seems like a yoke. From my non-MFA perspective, it seems like governance by debt: graduates accommodate market aesthetics in order to sell work, because otherwise the weight of the debt would destroy them. This seems like a big waste of time and an excuse to continue propping up white mediocrity, since the work itself is of less importance than the movement of capital and the continued precarization of art.

MAA:
As an "alt arts edu" model, home school exists as a casual corrective not only to this marketization of education and aesthetics, but as a corrective to previous alt arts edu models: whether it's a dearth of criticality or autonomy from the market, or a lack of distance learning opportunities, Victoria and I felt there was room for another method. The long-term goal is to build an archive showcasing the vernacular pedagogy and low-stakes, high-reward resource transfer that is so common to online friendships.

That being said, we owe a lot to those other models, so I want to name some names: BHQFU, Anton Vidokle's Night School, Conceptual Oregon Performance School, University of Trash. As well, home school is lucky to be a 2015 Precipice Fund grantee; this allows us access to equipment, labor payment, and other necessities in order to be able to provide streams of every home school event.

EF:
Your visual arts practice takes an ephemeral, non-art turn that I could see talked about as antagonistic to the idea of an art-object. Your day-to-day sculptural works are found "trash" that are re-collected, arranged and documented primarily through Instagram and your garageresidency Tumblr, which you began upon moving into a garage in Southeast Portland after a period of housing instability. How do you contextualize this process as art-making in the moment of creation and once the digital footprint is all that is left?

MAA:
I want to say "I don't contextualize it like that" but I'd be lying or something... First and foremost, I do it because I like it, regardless of whether context, discourse, and/or institutionality allow the labor to be legible as art.

[artist unknown]

Second, I want to be a cool art kid, but I'm not much of a maker. This means that regardless of my investment in reading certain aesthetic labors as art, at least to some extent what I do needs to be read this way for my contingent inclusion in ~ the Discourse ~. "Luckily," this may actually be to my advantage: Paul Mann says in *The Theory-Death of the Avant Garde* that "the dematerialization of the art object is the refetishization of discourse." The non-artistic nature of aspects of my practice speak, at least in part, to this situation, in which language's power as value creator and impression management machine frame and validate aesthetic labor; I want my work to talk back to its framing, by its own dissolution or otherwise, not just mutely accommodate it. #goals

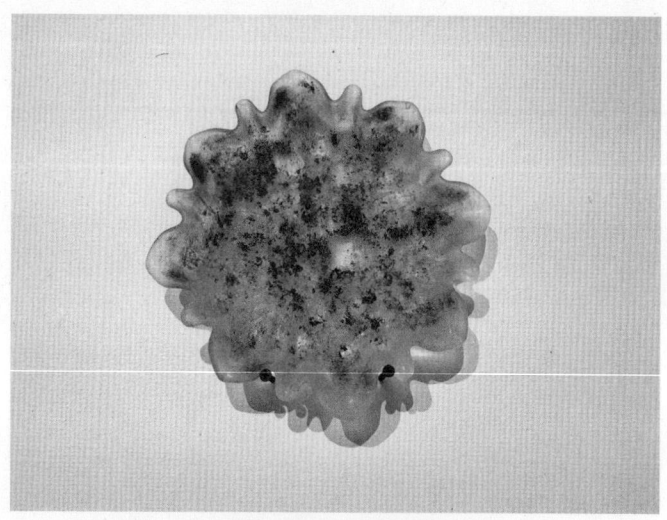

untitled, 2016. Glass, nails, ash.
For Remains at Reed College Feldenheimer Gallery,
with Erin Jane Nelson and fish narc

Third, when I moved into the garage around in 2013, I was thinking a lot about Brian Droitcour's critique of post-internet objects, which he says don't activate space, instead preening themselves for the camera. He states this pejoratively, but it made me think about the slippage between an ephemeral work and its documentation: is activating space something that a work inherently needs to do? Can this activation happen digitally (this question assumed the internet as a space, not a process, but still)?

Finally, I'm just going to copy and paste an artist statement I wrote when I got asked to write about my practice's relationship to "social justice," because it feels like you're coyly asking about politicization:

I am a poet and artist who is cruising dystopia. I work with found text, ephemeral sculpture, photography, and writing to ask the question: what does it mean for something to fail to be art, and how is value involved? My process is precarious; I use whatever is at hand in a given moment, operating on the basis of magical thinking. My work addresses language, the pretensions of the white Left, the relationship between debt and community, and the ritual aspects of aesthetics. I am less interested in an autonomous art practice or the creation of value, and more interested in working from the position of having been post-apocalyptic since 1492, to interrogate the trap of visibility and the conditions of affective and aesthetic legibility in a world where bodies of color like mine, trans or cis, have more value as a carcass-turned-hashtag than as a person. The deployment of failure in the neoliberal marriage of precarity and scarcity interests me on many fronts, partly due to my specific embodiment as a transgender nonbinary Dominican immigrant: failing to be a man or woman, failing to be Dominican or American, failing to be Black, white, latinx. Along with identity this extends to more general concerns about precarity: for example, the didactic role of documentation with respect to ephemeral art, or the precarity and unwaged nature of so much art labor as the art world and art education continues to professionalize. As well, my work and life would not be possible without the shelter of the vernacular, the hard love of family, the generative capacity of negativity, and the benevolence of my ancestors.

QUESTIONNAIRE:

Age: 24

Location: Santo Domingo -> Bronx -> Portland, OR

**How/when did you begin working
creatively with technology?**
In 5th grade, each classroom got an iMac and I remember loving to write bad short stories on the one in mine in a cursive font. This was also the year my northwest Bronx neighborhood became flooded with promotional AOL trial discs; some of the cases were wood, some plastic. I loved to empty the plastic ones, fill them with objects, and slip new covers into the laminate. I also used these cases to package and sell a rap album I made in 7th grade (I used to make beats with Anvil Studio, but switched to FL Studio). That same year, I remember being very active on a *Magic: The Gathering* forum, and creating cards and game mechanics with various other members.

While I definitely frequented AOL chatrooms, fan forums, and other contexts, what addicted me to digital sociality was the chatrooms in SoulSeek, a p2p file sharing program which differed from other programs I knew of in one crucial, almost erotic way: the ability to browse someone's home computer file structure. This felt quite intimate. I feel like I've been chasing that sensation ever since, despite knowing now that the internet has become increasingly corporatized (and was back then, just less successfully).

**Where did you go to school?
What did you study?**
I received my BA in Linguistics from Reed College in 2014. My thesis was on Spanish pronoun-like elements called clitics.

What do you do for a living or what occupations have you held previously?
I have worked as a transcriptionist, SEO copywriter, personal assistant, janitor, research assistant, small press managing editor, and babysitter. I currently work as an IT Compliance analyst and administrative assistant.

What does your desktop or workspace look like? (Pics or screenshots please!)

GAMING THE SYSTEM: MONGREL'S "BLACKLASH" AGAINST STEREOTYPES IN 1990s VIDEOGAMES

This essay accompanies the presentation of Mongrel's *BlackLash* as a part of the online exhibition Net Art Anthology.

At the turn of the millennium and even earlier, games had a much greater impact on American culture than contemporary art. Unlike other mediums, games have an interactive dimension that allows for deep affective investment. No surprise then that at the horizon of gaming's figurative puberty, artists were playing with the medium: among others, there was Manetas's *Flames* (1997), Thomson and Craighead's *Space Invaders*-format meditation on authorship *Trigger Happy* (1998), Natalie Bookchin's Borges adaption *Intruder* (1999), Dutch collective JODI's disorienting, minimalist *Wolfenstein 3D mod SOD* (1999), and British collective Mongrel's *BlackLash* (1998). This latter work was particularly important for its repudiation of utopian virtuality, examining the specific context of gaming and its prominent stereotyping of Blackness.

1998 marked a horizon of vast potential for gaming: in the sixth console generation, technological advancements allowed for more realistic graphics, and the astronomic rise of game sales broadened the market, ushering in a shift in focus toward teen and adult gamers rather than kids. The hacker ethos of the 1980s was merging with gaming culture, evidenced by modding communities for games like *Half-Life* (1998) and the beginnings of a now-flourishing indie game market. Nintendo's family-friendly grip on the industry had loosened, allowing new players like Sony and Microsoft to step in and begin establishing their own gaming empires.

However, these developments did not address the problems of earlier gaming ideology, leading to the new horizon—in many cases—simply replicating these issues. For example, the early waves of gaming in the US were predominantly white: white male developers created white male characters for presumed white male players. Avatars of color only appeared as stereotypes and punching bags. Orpheus Hanley, a Black American composer and sound designer who worked at Midway Games, describes the situation: "In the 80's and 90's you never saw Black characters. If there were Black ones, they would get beat up, really whumped so fast, before they had time to get into character."[1]

Taking cues from modding aesthetics of the time but with an eye toward the historical precedents of the new horizon of gaming, the British collective Mongrel[2] inverted the paradigm Hanley describes with their 1998 Macintosh game, *BlackLash*. Instead of

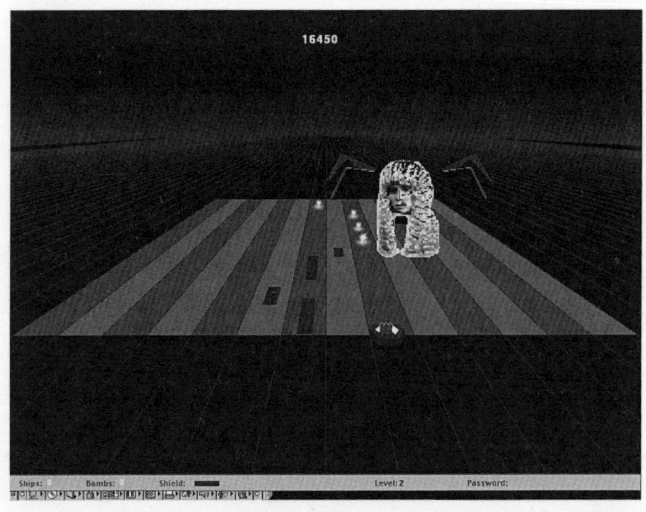

Screenshot from *BackLash*.

---

1. Marriott 1999
2. Mongrel was formed around 1995 by Graham Harwood, Matsuko Yokokoji, and Richard Pierre Davis, with Mervin Jarman joining later. Harwood and Yokokoji met at Guildhall University; the others met at Artec, the Arts Technology Centre in London

making Black characters bear the brunt of physical violence, the game features a Black protagonist doling out the attacks against a variety of antiblack aggressors. *BackLash* finds the slippage between the "hood" and the "information superhighway," excavating the market-driven stereotyping of Blackness in gaming and virtuality to "battle the forces of evil that plot to convict or eliminate you from the streets."[3]

Working from 1995-2008, Mongrel worked to fuse "a challenge to the conception of cybercultures as "race neutral" with a corresponding refusal of the contemporary invocation of a multiculturalism-beyond-conflict."[4] Through sardonic irony, unauthorized software modification, hacktivism, false corporations, and other forms of culture jamming, the group pilloried the hegemonic ideologies of post-Thatcher Britain and celebrated "the methods of an 'ignorant' and 'filthy' London street culture."[5] In vernacular aesthetics they saw not only the potential for greater reach but deeper critique. Their foray into gaming was no different: Mongrel member Richard Pierre-Davis states that Mongrel "hacked another game and created a game called *BlackLash*...I was fed up with companies making Black games with no relation to Black people whatsoever."[6]

Released for Macintosh in 1998, *BlackLash* is a mod of a 1995 Mac game called *Macattack* in which you maneuver a spaceship in various pseudo-3D planes divided into lanes, shooting enemies to score as many points and survive as long as possible. In

---

3. http://www2.tate.org.uk/netart/mongrel/home/faqs/ns.htm
4. McGahan 2004: 46
5. Lovink 1998
6. Everett 2001: 109

BlackLash, the spaceship is replaced with four Black stereotypes as playing options: professional, crime-lord, lover, dry-cleaner. Enemy ships become "white wigged judges, cops, hypodermic needles, Ku-Klux-Klan heads, Nazi spiders,"[7] and others with roles in the oppression and violence against Black people. Dated 7 November 2070, the game copy states:

> The filth is still in command of society and the streets, making sure only the selected few can escape the shit hole. The authorities have unleashed their law enforcers to crack down on the undesirables and maintain control of the streets contaminating all areas with guns and drugs. Here is your chance to kick some arse and annihilate the powers that be and smack them into the next millennium.

The game also features a presumably appropriated Wu-Tang Clan soundtrack.

Like some other examples of videogame art at the time, *BlackLash* foregoes 3D realism, instead sourcing a title that was already ancient in gaming terms. Not only does this properly situate modding culture in an older, originary hacker ethos; by juxtaposing earlier gaming aesthetics with the heavily stereotyped nonwhite characters in the gaming landscape of 1998, Mongrel suggested a connection between the two which begs exploring. This older focus also ties the new wave of gaming and market-driven stereotyping to the unacknowledged contribution of non-white youth to the early gaming boom: as Greg Tate argues, heavy gameplay by young Black and Latino men in late seventies arcades was a direct contributor to the flourishing of the gaming industry.[8] If

---

7. Nideffer 2003
8. Dery 1994: 209

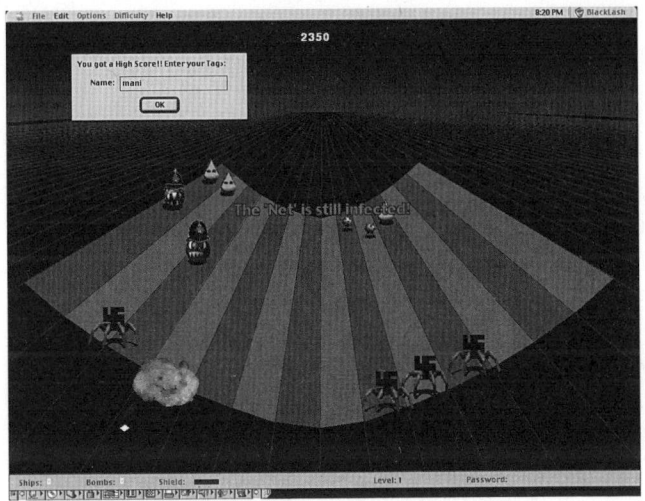

The author losing on level 1 with 2350 points.

the stereotypes in games in the two decades that followed were some sort of conciliation in light of this, they were a huge failure, and the tech-driven utopianism of turn-of-century gaming simply continued to erase this unacknowledged contribution in the face of an increasingly diverse consumer base.

The earlier-mentioned 1999 article that quotes Hanley—a high-profile *New York Times* piece by Michel Marriott—frames the time of its writing as a paradigm shift where in the sixth generation of games,

> as a result of a series of rapid developments both technological and sociological, Blacks and members of other minorities are being represented in more and more computer games as fully realized characters... In a broad range of new

releases like Wu-Tang: Shaolin Style, Urban Chaos, Shadow Man, and Ready 2 Rumble Boxing, nonwhite characters are stars rather than bit players.[9]

In Marriott's understanding, the horizon of greater graphical and conceptual realism also meant a more equitable ecology of visual difference in games.

However, in reality nonwhite characters in games at the time continued and exacerbated stereotypes of old gaming, ranging from the comic relief of *Ready 2 Rumble*'s infamous Afro Thunder—actually modeled on Orpheus Hanley[10]—to the violently absurd, such as the protagonist of Acclaim's *Shadow Man*, a Black cab driver who has been turned into a "supreme zombie-warrior slave."[11] A 2011 survey of 150 games found that 100% of Black male characters were portrayed as either athletic, violent, or both.[12] As well, then and now, games generally portrayed women as nubile objects to save, fuck, kill, or fulfill some other "gameplay" function.[13]

Journalist and media executive Adam Clayton Powell III, who at the time was vice president of technology and programming at the Freedom Forum, was quoted in Marriott's article describing the computer games industry and its prevalence of stereotyped characters as "high-tech blackface."[14] Given that games aspire to profitability, we might conclude, like scholar of digital culture

---

9. Ibid.
10. Marriott 1999
11. As described by *Shadow Man* game designer Guy Miller.
12. Burgess et al 2011
13. The extensive work of journalist and media critic Anita Sarkeesian details this well for the contemporary gaming context.
14. Marriott 1999

and Black cinema Anna Everett, that such high-tech blackface and other encrypted racist and orientalist messaging have a profit motive along with their naturalization of hegemonic ideology.[15] These flat Black avatars are easy ways to spice up the visual aspect of games for a presumed white audience hungry for "safe" encounters with otherness.

Of course, the problem of "high-tech blackface" will continue as long as game development is primarily white.[16] While white developers may sometimes meticulously develop full-fledged nonwhite characters—like the acclaimed half-French, half-Haitian Aveline in *Assassin's Creed III: Liberation* (2012), set in 18th-century Louisiana—the critical nuance of lived difference will always escape even the most thorough research. Moreover, given the outcry in recent years at games like *FIFA 17* featuring a Black protagonist[17] or survival game Rust randomly assigning race and gender to players,[18] it is clear gamers value choice more than difference itself, chafing at being forced to play as non-white, non-male characters. The putatively safe encounter with difference promised by virtual identity flux becomes foreclosed for the white male audience when difference, as it is in reality, is not a costume choice but a random, imposed fact. Likewise, *BlackLash*—despite its intentions—is not free of the "white touch."

---

15. Everett 2001: 124
16. The International Game Developers Association found in 2015 that out of nearly 3,000 surveyed developers only 3% of game developers were Black, while 76% were white; 75% of all surveyed were men.
17. https://news.vice.com/article/people-are-mad-they-have-to-play-a-black-character-in-fifa-17
18. http://steamed.kotaku.com/rust-chooses-players-race-for-them-things-get-messy-1693426299

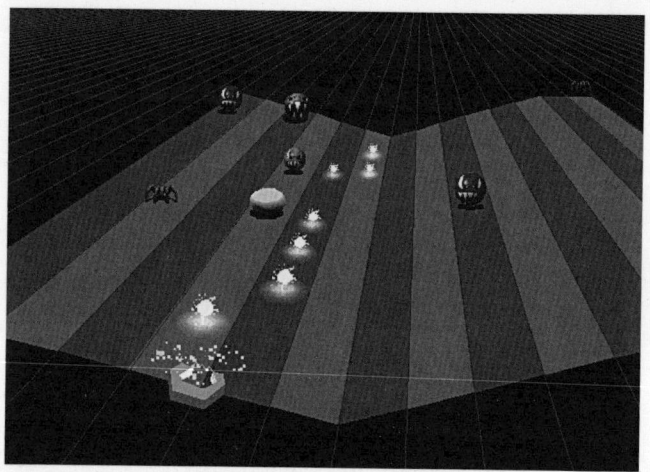

Screen shot from MacAttack.

Indeed, the perpetual forward motion of the game's tubular vector spaces is redolent of the dominant metaphor for the digital at the time: the "information superhighway," and the enemies embody the insidious ideologies crawling around in it. The game points to the violence hidden in utopian metaphors of seamless connection, speed, and ahistorical globality, as well as the resilience required to navigate this naivete. Even at low difficulty levels, the game does call for some dexterity, particularly due to the KKK enemies: upon being shot or reaching the end of the vector space, each Klan member hatches into two Nazi spiders which land on adjacent columns of the space. At higher difficulty levels, even a slight misstep can lead to an absurd proliferation of Nazi spiders at the screen edge. This speaks to the stickiness of these violent ideologies, which in the game's universe (and likely in ours) are thriving in 2070.

BlackLash leverages the market logic of stereotypes in the industry to gamify the nightmare deep at the heart of white multiculturalism: Black retribution. However, this gamification also points to the fetish for critical Black aesthetics in progressive culture. This fear perversely generates a performative identification with Blackness to erase one's complicity in antiblack violence—as Meryl Streep put it when asked about Black representation in film, "we're all Africans."[19] *BlackLash* also points to the origins of high-tech blackface in older virtual aesthetics. While performative identity morphing was a common aspect of 1990s digital culture,[20] the political reality of lived difference was rarely acknowledged, rendering moot whatever idealistic liberatory potential to be claimed in cyber-fluidity. As such, *BlackLash* seems implicitly aimed toward a white audience, asking it to confront its stereotypes about Black men, the marginalized condition of Black America, and the mainstream representation of the "inner city."

Despite being billed as "the game the streets have been waiting for," the necessary affective investment in the stereotypical character options is only really potentially subversive for a white gamer, since for a Black gamer this is just another instance of being forced to identify with a stereotype (even a super random one like the dry-cleaner). Notably, however, these were not present in the demo version I played, and the promise of these tropes upon payment for the full game is perhaps a wry comment on the commodification of identity. And of course, the potential gratification of shooting the sordid cast of enemies has not aged well in the context of nihilistic sandbox games like the *GTA* series, where the premise is being able to "do whatever you want." Nev-

---

19. https://www.theguardian.com/film/2016/feb/11/meryl-streep-berlin-film-festival-diversity-were-all-africans-really
20. McGahan 2004: 9

ertheless, *BlackLash* is an early attempt to inject explicitly political content into a game from either the industry or the art world, presaging the current climate of criticality in both.

We can assume Mongrel could have modded *Half-Life* to execute the *BlackLash* concept if they wanted. But the choice to work with a vector graphics game likely made things easier and faster; it also allows the audience to reflect on the ways the supposed development of gaming only replicates its older, originary stereotypes as ostensibly "blacks and members of other minorities are being represented in more and more computer games as fully realized characters."[21] More realistic virtual environments are only a new skin for the same tropes, more and more advances in high-tech blackface.

The speed of deployment for *BlackLash* was important because the game was a facet of larger Mongrel projects at the time. With

Image from poster advertising Mongrel's *Natural Selection* (1999), a search engine that illuminated the omnipresence of white supremacist material online. A component of the National Heritage campaign.

---

21. Marriott 1999

the hacktivist re-education project *Natural Selection* (1999), Mongrel disrupted various popular search engines such that when users typed in racial slurs, they were directed to a small network of art projects tackling new technologizations of racism, including Mongrel's own *BlackLash* and *Heritage Gold* (1998), Mervin Jarman's Yardie *Immigration Advisor* (1998), Hakim Bey's *Islam and Eugenics* (1997), and others. Further, *Natural Selection* was part of an even larger Mongrel project, *National Heritage*, named after the UK's arts funding allocation department. *National Heritage* began in 1997 and consisted of "street poster / newspaper publication, a WWW search engine, and a gallery installation"[22] to show the ways that, as Graham Harwood states, "racial dichotomy is the heritage of the nation... and multiculturalism is their excuse for keeping power."[23]

BlackLash thus operates both as a standalone product and as a facet of a wider agitprop project using tools of digital and mass media to disseminate anti-hegemonic content. Working in inherently commodified forms like videogames, search engines, and consumer applications, the collective critiqued the ways that putatively radical technologies easily worked in service of national and corporate projects. As well, they embodied the problem of radicality: the necessity of simultaneously imagining alternate worlds and using all available tools, since as Joseph Beuys put it you cannot wait for a tool without blood on it. In all of their projects, Mongrel committed to a refusal to provide easily digestible solutions to the violence of multiracial global capitalism, opting instead to thrust audiences into interactive networked and software experiences to encounter our own investments in the power structure, and maybe even have fun in our self-critique.

---

22. http://v2.nl/archive/works/national-heritage
23. Lovink 1998

BIBLIOGRAPHY

Burgess, M. C. R., Dill, K. E., Stermer, S. P., Burgess, S. R., & Brown, B. P. 2011. Playing with prejudice: The prevalence and consequences of racial stereotypes in videogames. *Media Psychology* 14.3: 289-311.

Dery, Mark (ed). 1994. *Flame Wars: The Discourses of Cyberculture*. Durham, NC: Duke University Press.

Duggan, Maeve. 2015. *Games and Gamers*. Pew Research Center.

Everett, Anna. 2001. *Digital Diaspora: A Race for Cyberspace*. Albany: SUNY Press.

Lovink, Geert. 1998. National Heritage and the Natural Selection Search Engine: Interview with

Harwood and Matsuko of Mongrel (London) {AT} OpenX, Ars Electronica. Nettime.

Marriott, Michel. 1999. Blood, Gore, Sex and Now: Race. *The New York Times*.

McGahan, Christopher. 2004. *Race-ing for Cybercultures: The Performance of Minoritarian Cultural Work as Challenge to Presumptive Whiteness on the Internet*. PhD Diss., New York University.

Nideffer, Robert F. 2003. *Game Engines as Creative Frameworks*. Self-published.

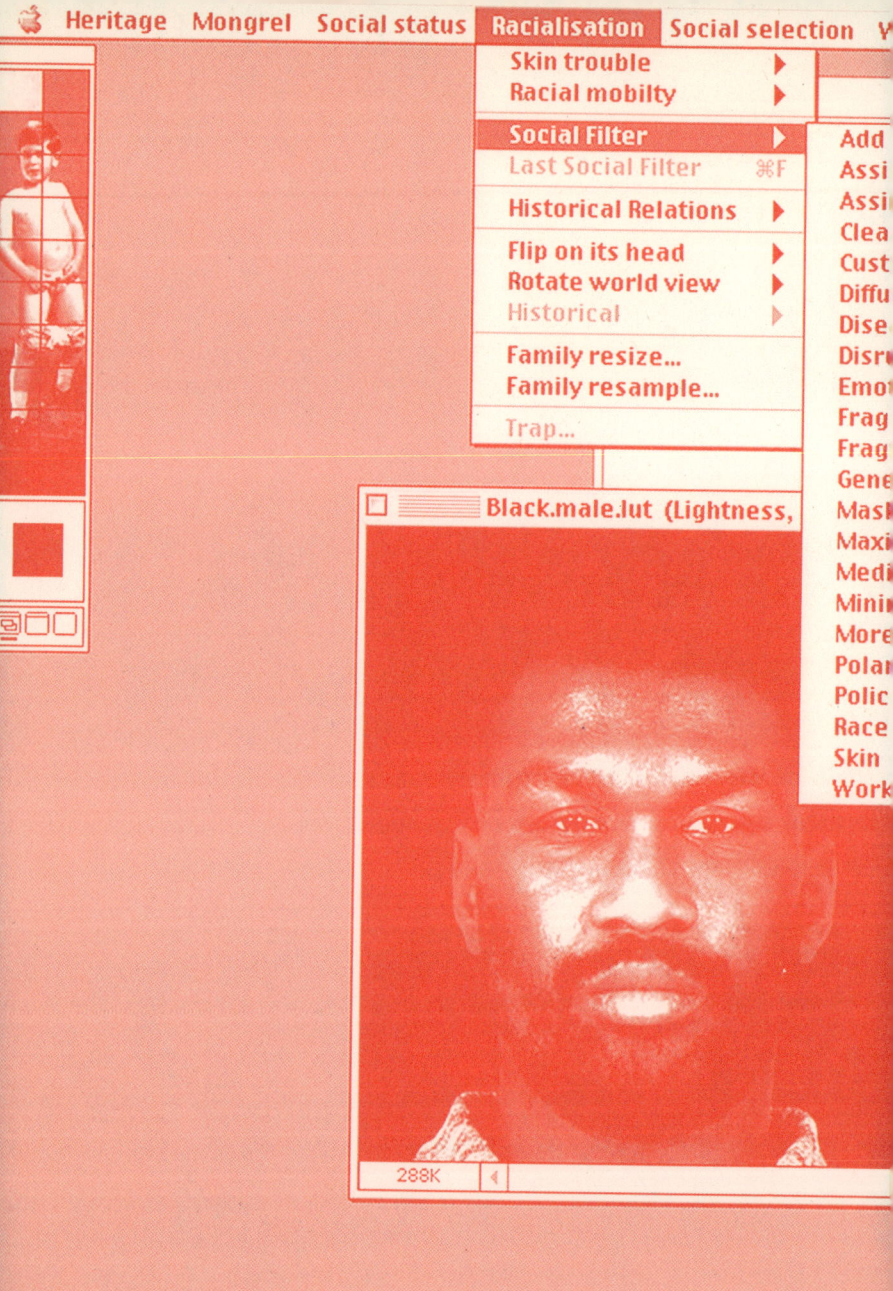

7:05 AM

tageGoldSoft

hd

Unix

disk   65.1 MB available

Read Me

ore

Ines...

...

Blur...

ss

ss...

...

THINK DIFFERENT: MONGREL'S "HERITAGE GOLD" AND THE COMMODIFICATION OF IDENTITY

This essay accompanies the presentation of Mongrel's *Heritage Gold* as a part of the online exhibition Net Art Anthology.

The past two decades saw the full corporatization of the internet, as well as the rhetorical adoption by nation states and multinational corporations of cybertropes like fluidity, mobility, and recombinancy.[1] Early post-identity cyber-utopianism gave way to Anonymous's nihilist hacktivism, Amazon Prime's frictionless consumerism, and the generalized reification of antiblackness and misogyny once thought so escapable via virtuality. Far from engendering a world "beyond identity and individuality and thus beyond the reach of commodification,"[2] digital technology has generated new ways to subsume sociality into the violence of capital. These novel structures of informatic domination are heavily "inflected by the values, cultures, power systems, and institutional orders within which it is embedded,"[3] showing that post-identity rhetoric only aids the commodification of identity at the expense of the marginalized.

Image courtesy of v2.nl.

Identity morphing was a major facet of 1990s cyberculture,[4] but whatever liberation or cross-demographic empathy folks expected only manifested as an identity tourism that widened the gap between the marginalized and the hegemon performing otherness.[5] Today, the privileged can continue the ludic tradition of

---

1. McGahan 2004: 42
2. Hansen 2004: 172
3. Sassen 2002: 109
4. MCGahan 2004: 9
5. Nakamura 2002: 57

early post-identity cyber aesthetics, but a seamless objectification and policing of marginalized people between virtual and flesh space has been achieved—with harassment, criminalization, and surveillance continuing to be the norm for Black and Brown people. Meanwhile, corporations preach diversity in one breath and excuse their hiring and business practices with the other, repackaging the same utopianism of seamless connection and service for a born-digital market.

Just as blackface has been analyzed as a site for white men to project their class anxiety,[6] one can argue that early cyberculture's identity laboratory[7] was a similar projection, foreshadowing both the cagey egalitarian rhetoric of the "disruptive" corporate digital landscape and the hugely increased access to otherness the internet has provided.[8] The output of British collective Mongrel[9] proves instructive and prescient here. Working from 1995-2008, they took the piss out of the administration of multicultural policy which burgeoned in post-Thatcher Britain (and which today serves as a corporate marketing staple) through sardonic irony, unauthorized software modification, false corporations, and other forms of culture jamming. Self-identified celebrants of "the methods of an 'ignorant' and 'filthy' London street culture,"[10] Mongrel worked to fuse "a challenge to the conception of cybercultures as 'race neutral' with a corresponding refusal of the contemporary invocation of a multiculturalism-beyond-conflict."[11]

---

7. McGahan 2004: 21
8. Where, for example, whites prefer communicating with nonwhite emoji.
9. Mongrel was formed in 1997 by Graham Harwood, Matsuko Yokokoji, and Richard Pierre Davis, with Mervin Jarman joining later. Harwood and Yokokoji met at Guildhall University; the others met at Artec, the Arts Technology Centre in London.
10. Lovink 1998
11. McGahan 2004: 46

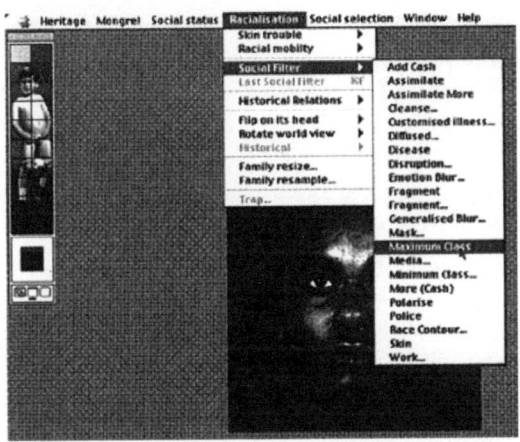

Screen shot from *Heritage Gold 1.0* via oldweb.today.

One work offers a trenchant analysis of the commodification of identity, playing off the British euphemism of "heritage" to mean white imperial patrimony:[12] *Heritage Gold*, released for Macintosh in 1998, is a parodic shareware mod of Adobe Photoshop 1.0 allowing users to alter their race and ancestry. With drop-down menus for modifying ethnic features, social mobility, prejudice, family size, assimilation, and more, the software promises to "transform [the user's] Heritage into personal works of art," touting itself as "the worldwide industry standard among dedicated diversity professionals."[13] The concept archly explicates how image editing software marketizes the cyber-utopian rhetoric of fluidity somehow engendering equity, or at least sameness, whateverness: "Why settle for the same old you?"

---

12. Gonzalez 2009
13. Archive snapshot of Heritage Gold page

Ostensibly the product of Mongrelsoft™, a mock corporation borrowing Apple's slogan "Think Different,"[14] the work satirizes the way the identity laboratory of 1990s cyberculture easily plays into corporate diversity rhetoric. As an example, the software cover and the "Activities" web page showcase *Heritage Gold*'s functionality by grafting a photograph of a baby Prince Charles with a postcard showing a dark-skinned baby poised to urinate, resulting in two babies—one with normatively Anglo features, and one with normatively Afro features. Of course, this baby's Blackness is primarily linguistic, since it could easily be Mediterranean or Middle Eastern.

The copy states the Prince Charles edit "really made us think: "What would the world be like today if we in England had a black Monarch?" Just maybe, there wouldn't be so many wars..."[15] By positioning difference, in particular Blackness, as absolution, the web copy paradoxically implies a situation in which the fruits of British empire remain without their sordid history of slavery, colonization, and imperialism. The satire skewers the idea that a multicultural citizenship or power structure could in any way mitigate the violence of capitalism.

The software cover further parodies this diversity-beyond-conflict with a modified British Royal Arms, notably replacing the lion's head with a golliwog head, and the unicorn's head with what appears to be either a toff[16] or an archetypal fool. In this way, the work prefigures analyses of heritage and marginality such as that of David Joselit, who argues that contemporaneity

---

14. McGahan 2004: 51
15. Ibid.
16. A derogatory term for the aristocracy and landed gentry.

Software cover for *Heritage Gold 1.0* (MongrelsoftTM, 1998).

governs marginal practitioners by claiming their debt to modernism, mitigated by the commercial and conciliatory functions that individual heritage can serve for national prestige and market diversification.[17]

Inside its satirical world, *Heritage Gold* is perfect for both the "diversity professional" who often finds herself needing to "colorize" a photo of white workers, and the casual user looking to goof off or roleplay. While similar software artworks might naively claim visual morphing "allows us to move beyond differences and arrive at sameness,"[18] *Heritage Gold* focuses on the assump-

---

17. Heritage and Debt, Walker Art Center, Feb 2015.
18. Nancy Burson describing her project *Human Race Machine* (2000). The artwork algorithmically morphs the input user portrait into a set of racially distinct replicas similar to Heritage Gold, except with utopian post-difference aims.

tion that end users would want to alter their racial identities at all. This desire reveals the presumptive whiteness of cyber, where difference is a commodity to be donned when pleasurable and/or profitable. As such, the early 90s identity laboratory was inherently commodified and premised on the long history of unconditional white access to all facets of otherness, flattening the violence of difference to circulation.

In this way, *Heritage Gold* not only predicts the post-fact, retouched reality we live in today, but excavates the always already phobic impulse of a fantasy of difference which centers whiteness as its condition of possibility, closely mirroring eugenicist Jose Vasconcelos's concept of *mestizaje*: "the white race has brought the world to a state in which all human types and cultures will be able to fuse with each other," organizing "the moral and material basis for the union of all men... the fruit of all the previous ones and amelioration of everything past."[19] The internet *itself* could stand in for this notion, exemplifying how whiteness attempts to erase its constitutive violence by positioning itself as a transcultural connective tissue.

The flipside of whiteness's putative neutrality is the speculative categorizing of visual difference which, in the context of *Heritage Gold*, is best exemplified by Francis Galton's composite portraiture technique: splicing together many faces via multiple exposures on the same photographic plate, Galton aimed to determine both the "typical" face and the criminality, intelligence, and other affective qualities of various facial features.[20]

---

19. Vasconcelos 1997: 9. Vasconcelos is speaking of his notion of the mestizo or cosmic race, but the parallels to 90s cyber-utopian rhetoric are striking.
20. Galton 1878

Cover of the November 1993 issue of TIME magazine.

The libidinal economy of such physiognomic speculation belies anxiety about control, and *Heritage Gold* promises that "many powerful ethnic features are yours to *command* through our new, even easier-to-use interface" (emphasis added).

Granted, *Heritage Gold* may be at home skewering a wide set of sanitized diversity discourses, but it doesn't provide any solution to the commodification of difference, only another experience of it. We should take care not to view this as ressentiment;[21] rath-

---

21. Gonzalez 2009: 54

er, the work's lack of reconciliation exemplifies the rapidity with which real or imagined radical potential gets subsumed into capital. Just as the project "critiques the notion that the national culture is susceptible to touching up...to mask over the bases for conflict among inequitably empowered social actors,"[22] it shows how the early digital identity laboratory and its descendants easily play into this masking of conflict.

The same rhetoric of fluidity and post-identity is present at the level of the national project and the zeitgeist, and Heritage Gold calls for end users of all levels of digital literacy to think more critically about their participation in the "touching up" of social problems and the perpetuation of oppression.[23] Its call remains as urgent today. Representations of difference are neither salve nor salvo in global informatic capitalism; they are the same as any other platform for deepening the subsumption of all sociality into the dictums of western value. With *Heritage Gold*, Mongrel offers a sandbox for exploring our own affective investments in antiblack fantasies of commodified difference and whiteness as transcultural connective tissue. These violent delights have violent ends.

---

22. McGahan 2004: 53
23. It's also worth noting that the project speaks to the long list of art projects involving white people pretending to be other races or creating people of other races, such as Joe Scanlan's invented Black woman Donelle Woolford. In the context of utopianism, what does it mean that the capitalist has an easier time inventing an *other* rather than engaging with actual oppressed people?

BIBLIOGRAPHY

Galton, Francis. 1878. Composite portraits. *Journal of the Anthropological Institute of Great Britain and Ireland*, 8: 132–142.

González, Jennifer. 2009. The Face and the Public: Race, Secrecy, and Digital Art Practice. *Camera Obscura* 70, Vol 24, No. 1. Duke University Press.

Hansen, Mark. 2004. Digitizing the Racialized Body; or, The Politics of Universal Address. *Substance* 33: 107–33.

Lovink, Geert. 1998. National Heritage and the Natural Selection Search Engine: Interview with Harwood and Matsuko of Mongrel (London) {AT} OpenX, Ars Electronica. nettime.

McGahan, Christopher. 2004. *Race-ing for Cybercultures: The Performance of Minoritarian Cultural Work as Challenge to Presumptive Whiteness on the Internet*. PhD Diss., New York University.

McPherson, Tara. 2000. "I'll Take My Stand in Dixie-Net": White Guys, the South and Cyberspace. *Race in Cyberspace*. Eds. Beth Kolko, Lisa Nakamura, & Gilbert Rodman. New York: Routledge.

Nakamura, Lisa. 2002. *Cybertypes: Race, Ethnicity and Identity on the Internet*. New York: Routledge.

Roediger, David. 1991. *The Wages of Whiteness: Race and the Making of the American Working Class*. New York: Verso.

Sassen, Saskia. 2002. Mediating Practices: Women With/In Cyberspace. *Living with Cyberspace: Technology and Society in the 21st Century*. Eds. John Armitage & Joanne Roberts. London: Continuum: 109-119.

Vasconcelos, Jose. 1997 [1925]. *The Cosmic Race*. Baltimore: John Hopkins University Press.

AGAINST THE SUPREMACY OF THOUGHT

Do you remember when people misheard the words "fuck that" on the chorus of Kendrick Lamar's "A.D.H.D." as "fuck thought?" Well, fuck thought. Kind of. Let's talk about it.

1.
REANALYZING THE THOUGHT FETISH

By means of "lack of reason"—with religion, language, appearance, and other aspects serving as a litmus—the animalization of Black and Brown people has been a critical tool of domination, invented to justify the white conquest, genocide, slavery, and other violence that engendered the contemporary.

What does it mean, then, that art today prizes thinking and the aesthetics of thought such as criticality, divestment from the sensory, and a demeanor of philosophical objectivity? The white West used these very criteria to dehumanize the global south and facilitate Euro expansion; in a specifically aesthetic context, modernism itself was premised on the spoils of imperial conquest.

Despite clarion calls of posthumanism, it is possible to excavate an exclusionary humanism in the fetishism for "objective philosophical thought" in contemporary art which preserves the modernist dynamic of treating Black and Brown people and aesthetics as raw material. We can recalibrate our definitions of art from the contemplation and production of the beautifully useless and self-referential. A continued utilitarian project of the violent subsumption of non-white aesthetics is possible through reading Allan Kaprow's concept of post-art in the context of the Middle Passage and its afterlife.

2.
THE CONTEMPORARY

David Joselit defines the contemporary as a mode of aesthetic governance relegating marginal practitioners into a position of debt to modernism. For Joselit, this imposition of debt mirrors governance by debt in neocolonialism, rendering what he calls heritage or local context merely a dividend of debt, serving to diversify the art market and globalize its structural tropes (such as painterly abstraction, the white cube, the biennial, etc).[1]

---

1. Joselit, "Heritage and Debt" (lecture, Mack Lecture Series, Walker Art Center, Minneapolis, December 3, 2014), February 12, 2015.
2. As part of Home School—a free pop-up art school I co-facilitate in Portland—I taught a class called *Contemporaneity: building a better white supremacy*, which further explores these ideas.
3. "I call 'standard' the aesthetics whose principles (1) are recognized and accepted, across a number of variations, by institutional and academic communities and which thus constitute the object of confirmed knowledges; (2) whose principles define either a foundation for art or a philosophical description of art or, more generally, a normality and a normativity; which is to say (3) a determinism of the reciprocal causality of art and of philosophy. It poses well known questions of the type "What is art?" "What is the essence of art?" "What can art do?" and it believes it can answer these questions with certainty. In accordance with these questions,

Joselit's analytic is useful for unearthing not only the originary violence of modernism with respect to Black and Brown aesthetics, but also the ways the contemporary continues this project of subsumption.[2] Aesthetic governance by debt allows the increasingly marketized art world to commoditize difference and deploy it for its own ends, whether financial, nationalist, or otherwise.

Yoked under modernism, marginal artists must assimilate to standard aesthetics[3] and allow themselves to be deployed in service of institutionality. At a deeper level, aesthetic governance by debt allows art to deny modernism's own constitutive debt to Black and Brown aesthetics, which it used as raw material to shirk the constraints of earlier white art such as three-point perspective and objecthood.

The contemporary is an echo of modernism, it continues the edict of modernism while developing new forms of governance over marginalized artists.

3.
THE END OF ART

In the afterlife of conceptualism, thinking overcame and reframed making, and embodied a Hegelian assumption of teleological human evolution, such that Western society has outgrown

---

standard aesthetics describes the styles, forms and historical epochs of art in a broadly realist manner, for it believes it is possible to define both art and philosophy." Laruelle 2012.

4. Hegel, Hegel's *Aesthetics: Lectures on Fine Arts*, Vol. 1, 10. With respect to art, Hegel focuses on the contemplation of beauty, but for our purposes a tautological definition of art as whatever is called art works fine.

the stage at which art is the supreme mode of our knowledge of the Absolute. Hegel says "We have got beyond venerating works of art as divine and worshipping them... Thought and reflection have spread their wings above fine art."[4]

During Western industrialization, art's dependence on the sensory caused it to fall behind thought as the highest vocation and prime engine of knowledge, whose "very essence... is to go from the observable to the non-observable, from the immediate to the mediate."[5] For Hegel, human cultural developments like art and religion are vestigial forms, reflecting an older dependence on the sensory before the modern mastery of nature represented by industry.

For Hegel's teleology, art is over, but it remains a necessary step in human development: aesthetic contemplation and production indicate the gradient between human and non-human, setting the stage for reason to flourish. It is precisely the intimate revelry of the sensory which, when refined, allows for the philosophical flight into the immaterial, the theoretical, and the nonsensory. Without art, philosophy could not have risen.[6]

4.
THE CONCEPTUALIST GAMBIT

By dint of art's putative necessity to human development, conceptualism attempted to salvage the patrimony of Western art by ushering thought itself into the set of available artistic mediums.

---

5. Kaminsky, *Hegel on Art: An Interpretation of Hegel's Aesthetics*, 8.
6. Kaminsky, *Hegel on Art: An Interpretation of Hegel's Aesthetics*, 27.
7. Kaprow, *Essays on the Blurring of Art and Life*, 102.

From this lowered position, modernist aesthetics worked to expand the boundaries of what could be institutionalized as art. Conceptualism went further, and deployed the autonomous inutility of the art object inherited from modernism to show how, as Allan Kaprow states, "art has served as an instructional transition to its own elimination by life."[7]

While this may have partly emerged from idealistic notions of thought as medium precluding subsumption into the commodity form, the result was that the subject and role of art—which for Kaprow was "the ritual escape of Culture"—simultaneously subsumed and supervened on the sociopolitical, becoming instead a kind of immaterial or diaphanous residue which could coat any imaginable life context. In modernism, the idea that anything could be art was scandalous, whereas in conceptualism, this indeterminacy became mundane.

With art more deeply yoked to culture, art became a toolkit for interacting with the lived conditions of humanity akin to a social science or school of thought. The modernist decline of art's primacy resulted in the simultaneous expansion of art to whatever; the reduction of art to commentary on world affairs and meta-comments on its own history; and the valorization of thought as the ideal medium for aesthetic practice in this new context.

Kaprow's concept of post-art exemplifies this, blurring the line between art and life since "nonart is more art than Art art."[8] Whatever a person wants to get out of art, life has more of it, and art's duty is to take on a managerial relationship to the sensory by

---

[8]. Kaprow, *Essays on the Blurring of Art and Life*, 98.

existing in a state of fluidity, even precarity—and in this ephemeral state it haunts life, it folds all life into it. With this vastly expanded aesthetic field, thought as artistic medium engenders a process of art mimicking the disciplines of thought—namely science and philosophy.

5.
AN OAK TREE (1973)

It is instructive to consider a work that exemplifies the conceptualist gambit of folding thought into the set of available artistic mediums, with its resultant valorization of reason and philosophical aesthetics.

Irish artist Michael Craig-Martin's *An Oak Tree* (1973) is a conceptual work consisting of a glass of water placed on a glass shelf 253 centimeters off the ground with an accompanying text.[9] The work was first shown at the Rowan Gallery in London, 1974. In Q&A format, the text explains the artist's process of "changing a glass of water into a full-blown oak tree without altering the accidents of the glass of water." The oak tree resulting from this metaphysical alteration "will not ever have any other form but that of a glass of water," and when pushed to answer the question of where the art is, Craig-Martin states in the text that this resultant oak tree is the art object.

An Oak Tree (1973) plays on the Aristotelian supremacy of essence over accident. The essence of the oak tree persists, de-

---

[9]. This text was at first was handed out as a leaflet but is generally wall-mounted behind glass today.

manuel arturo abreu. *An Oak Tree*, 2018.
Glass from Pietro Belluschi's Commonwealth Building, tap water from Open Signal Portland Community Media center. Dimensions variable.

spite all of the sensory evidence to the contrary. The ostensible transformation is not aesthetically accessible, and therefore the particular oak tree presented to the audience has no aesthetic dimension at all. Rather, the aesthetic dimension is entirely accidental to the essence which is intended for gallery display: the former is a glass of water, the latter is an oak tree.

The work also reflects the artist's Catholic upbringing, drawing on the concept of transubstantiation. At the last supper, "Jesus took bread, and when he had given thanks, he broke it and gave it to his disciples, saying, 'take and eat; this is my body.' Then he took a cup, and when he had given thanks, he gave it to them, saying, 'Drink from it, all of you. This is my blood of the covenant, which is poured out for many for the forgiveness of sins.'"[10]

At communion, Catholics ceremonially consume a cracker and wine to signify the bread and wine which at the last supper was, in essence, the flesh and blood of Christ—despite the accidents of the bread and wine. With this shade of meaning, the artist intends to "deconstruct the work of art in such a way as to reveal its single basic and essential element, belief that is the confident faith of the artist in his [sic] capacity to speak and the willing faith of the viewer in accepting what he [sic] has to say. In other words, belief underlies our whole experience of art."[11]

An Oak Tree (1973) is a fine example of the conceptualist gambit and its vaunting of thought: it simultaneously extricates itself from the abject sensory, and more deeply yokes itself to it (since after all of this metaphysical transformation from a glass of water into an oak tree, the sensory dimension still indicates only a glass of water). In dissecting the social contract between artist and audience, *it* speaks to contemporary art as a secularized iteration of an originally theological endeavor, one which served as a litmus for humanity.

It seems to be an impossible puzzle but it's easy to solve the Rubik's Cube using algorithms.

---

10. Matthew 26:26-28 NIV.
11. Craig-Martin, *Landscapes*, 20.

6.
CARTESIAN DUALISM AND ANTIBLACK ANIMALIZATION

The concept and value of thought in the West belie a desire for divestment from the ostensibly inferior world of sensory phenomena in line with Cartesian mind/body dualism, where bodies are organic machines, and only humans, with reason and language, have souls. As Descartes claims, non-human animals, are simply one more facet of nature ripe for use: "they have no mental powers whatsoever... it is nature which acts in them, according to the disposition of their organs; just as we see that a clock consisting only of ropes and springs can count the hours and measure time more accurately than we can in spite of all our wisdom."[12]

According to this idea, a body can only supercede the machinic laws of nature with rational thought; all else serves as the sandbox in which to perfect reason, living and breathing but nevertheless objectified. In this way, Cartesian dualism demonstrates that "the practical elaboration of making a commitment to humanity is inhumanism... humanism is by definition a project to amplify the space of reason,"[13] Humanism's project to expand the scope and analytic power of reason requires a corollary dehumanized faction to serve as its foil and ground of deployment.

Building on Cartesian dualism, Hegel argues that "in Negro life the characteristic point is the fact that consciousness has not yet attained to the realization of any substantial objective existence,

---

12. Descartes, *Discourse on the Method of Correctly Conducting One's Reason and Seeking Truth in the Sciences*, 48.
13. Negarestani, "The Labor of the Inhuman, Part II: The Inhuman."

... What we properly understand by Africa, is the Unhistorical, Undeveloped Spirit, still involved in the conditions of mere nature, and which had to be presented here only as on the threshold of the World's History."[14]

Hegel frames his mention of Africa as perfunctory, but his portrayal of Blackness as primordial is a necessary assumption for his teleological understanding of history, which evolves toward European reason. Hegel transfers Descartes" human/animal dichotomy to the realm of human difference, and positions Africa as an inhuman prehistory without thought in order to naturalize slavery and conquest in the "development" of the West.

7.
THE VIOLENCE OF MODERNISM

In art we find a similar process. It was through the animalization of Black and Brown people as lacking reason that white artists could render non-white lands, aesthetics, and bodies as raw material to modify and deploy in response to Western art history, both conceptually and materially. By confining Black bodies to what Orlando Patterson terms "social and ontological death," the West could render us simultaneously as the fungible cornerstones of its program, and as valueless vestiges of prehistory.[15]

---

14. Hegel, *The Philosophy of History*, 111-12, 117.

15. The work of Orlando Patterson, Hortense Spillers, Sylvia Wynter, Saidiya Hartman, and others lay the ground for the emergence of the Afropessimist texture of thought. The former's analytic shift of focus toward the position of the slave allowed for the work of Frank Wilderson III, Jared Sexton, Christina Sharpe, and others to build on arguments about the fungibility of the Black body in racial capitalism, the social and ontological death of Black life, and the structure of

As Murrell states, the stolen objects that served as the inspiration for modernism "were treated as artifacts of colonized cultures rather than as artworks, and held so little economic value that they were displayed in pawnshop windows and flea markets."[16]

Armed with the fruits of conquest, white art "developed" away from representation (and eventually objecthood entirely) by means of positing the supremacy of thought as surfing on colonial spoils. Picasso, for example, said "African sculptures had helped him to understand his purpose as a painter, which was not to entertain with decorative images, but to mediate between perceived reality and the creativity of the human mind."[17] The same tendency continues today, with Black and Brown life "inspiring" white art, with non-white artists strategically included to absolve the white cube and diversify the market.

In response to the squalor of phenomena, art turned the *lived* into solely a surface for thought: thinking itself is the best medium for art when the entire universe is accessible as source material, allowing a performative divestment from modernist values while simultaneously arguing for the value-neutral availability of its tools in a newly managerial aesthetic practice.

---

multiracial global antiblackness. A simultaneous analytic trend of "black optimism" ostensibly in contrast to Afropessimism is exemplified by the work of Fred Moten and others. However, Sexton convincingly argues that the two are not so distinct, as embodied in the paradox that "black social death is black social life." Both Afropessimism and Black optimism engage the impossible possibility of Black existence as such. Further, "the object of black studies is the aim of black studies," that is, the horizon of Black liberation from social and ontological death. Sexton continues: "The most radical negation of the antiblack world is the most radical affirmation of a blackened world. Afro-pessimism is 'not but nothing other than' black optimism" (Sexton, "Ante-Anti-Blackness: Afterthoughts").
16, 17. Murrell, "African Influences in Modern Art."

The vaunting of thought in the contemporary in which criticality is a prime currency can be read as an echo of Cartesian disavowal of the sensory. In various histories of conquest, this acts as a defensive response to the excavation of the violence of modernism, and of art history more generally. This is perfectly in line with the speculative turn in global financial capitalism and its various projects of governance by debt, brutal resource extraction, and sanitized diversity, all of which serve to conceal the constitutive violence of capitalism.

8.
LAROCHE'S POST-ART

In stark contrast to Hegelian notions of art and human development as embodied by conceptualism and its afterlife, Brooklyn artist Winslow Laroche's reading of post-art is useful for critiquing the supremacy and aesthetics of thought. For Laroche, art conceals the modernist debt to Black and Brown aesthetics. In a text-to-speech sound piece featured on the inaugural episode of *The Diamond Stingily Show* on Know-Wave, Laroche polemically states "All white art is Black face or Brown face and all white people are cops and lurking snitches."

He questions the post-artistic valorization of objects that fluidly move between commodified art and nugatory non-art—precisely the fungible position the slave occupies in the *longue durée* of the Middle Passage, situated there by an imaginary deprivation of reason. In light of slavery, such fluidity and spectacle as a "talking commodity" is old hat. Fred Moten disagrees with Marx that the talking commodity is an impossibility, given the reality of transatlantic African slavery.[18] Further, Black folks have long

---

[18]. Moten 2003: 6.

known all sociality and aesthetics are always already subsumed into the commodity form under capitalism.

Venerating post-art fluidity only conceals art history's antiblackness, conforming to the tradition wherein, as Keith Obadike states, "to many white artists, Blackness represents some kind of borderless excess, some kind of unchecked expression."[19] Just as Picasso was titillated by the spoils of African colonization, the ostensible supremacy of thought and the corresponding fluidity of aesthetic processes relies on the erasure of modernist violence.

Laroche allows us to argue that far from living in a time "after art," the West has not yet actually reached the conditions for art: all the West knows as "art" since the Enlightenment is an ecology of criteria for inclusion which relies on the colonial subsumption of Black and Brown aesthetics. From this vantage, all Western aesthetic developments simply serve to conceal this subsumption. Art objects are not useless contexts for the contemplation of timeless ideas like beauty or art itself; they work to continue the modernist project of treating non-whiteness as raw material for white speculation.[20]

The conditions for art as autonomous non-utilitarian endeavor will never emerge as long as art's erasure of its own debt to Black and Brown practice continues. Western aesthetic developments simply conceal the violence of modernism, betraying their anxious inability to come to terms with its reality. Autonomous inutility is simply a simultaneous escapism and market capitulation, a covertly useful endeavor of continuing modernist violence.

---

19. Keith Townsend Obadike, interview by Coco Fusco, in Mendi + Keith Obadike, September 9, 2001.
20. abreu, "Notes on the Garage Residency."

The supremacy of thought upholds this erasure of white debt. The West has expanded humanism to include everyone, marketizing reason and detaching it from European patrimony. In this sense, traditional conservatism—from which reason as litmus of humanity emerged, and which seeks to uphold traditional European values like racial superiority and slow culture—is at odds with market conservatism, which thrives on speed and welcomes any increase in profits including multiculturalism, which it recognizes can easily coexist with white supremacy.[21]

Consequently, Black artists, if we choose, can operate under the assumption that art owes us. We are the true inheritors of the fluidity between art and nonart. We don't need to make things or think or write or create value in any way for art's patrimony: our flesh was used to build it. But we should also recognize that our inclusion into white cubes is not enough. Such inclusion is the least to be done. We must advocate that "Art art" pay dues to the marginalized bodies of aesthetic practice it violently treated and treats as raw material, and return the stolen objects that haunt its institutions.

9.
#PAYBLACKTIME

It is instructive to consider an example that reflects Laroche's post-art concept. *#PAYBLACKTiME* is a project which multimedia Brooklyn artist Rafia Santana began on November 9th, 2016. The artist describes the project as a "white-money transference system that provides free meals via Seamless / GrubHub to Black + Brown folx across the North Americas."[22]

---

21. Sexton, *Amalgamation Schemes: Antiblackness and the Critique of Multiracialism*.
22. *$6,398.79 = Total orders and dollar amount for #PAYBLACKTiME as of December 26, 2016*.

Image courtesy Rafia Santana.

A description of the work reads: *All orders are paid for by the White Guilt Reparations Fund for white people who ask "What can I do?" during a time when we have heavily publicized evidence of their race's direct connection to the continuous suffering and disenfranchisement of Black / Brown people worldwide.*

In an interview with FELT Zine, Santana states that the project's name is "a play on the phrase 'Payback Time,' and also a demand to pay back black people for the hundreds of years of free labor and continuing trauma in the US alone. It is time to pay back / pay black." The project not only offers white audiences an easy way to make concrete change, it translates the call for reparations into a service answering a need anyone could understand—hunger—and brings the audience into the conversation of what America owes Black people.

When I asked via Facebook chat whether *#PAYBLACKTiME* was art, Santana responded that "I haven't thought of it specifically as art but everything I do is art I guess." In its banal fluidity between art and non-art, and its delegation of audience and aesthetics into potential financial utility in service of feeding Black and Brown people, *#PAYBLACKTiME* exemplifies Laroche's post-art. It rejects the modernist premise of art's autonomous uselessness, which is just complicity with white supremacy and a fantasy of escape from the constitutive violence of art and capitalism. *#PAYBLACKTiME* calls on its audience to recognize the aesthetic value in the concrete, useful act of paying for non-white people's food. Rendering aesthetics as utility reveals the covert utility of the modernist art object: the hoarding of resources stolen from conquest, which must be redistributed.

10.
WIKIAFRICA

This essay has concerned itself with the Middle Passage and its afterlife, but Africans who remained on their native lands also faced and continue to face violent colonization processes orthogonal to that of the New World.

Wikipedia is touted as a digital democratization of information, but it often exhibits mob mentality, and its acceptance requirements can be exclusionary of information that does not fit the dominant paradigm. In particular, Wikipedia echoes the general lack of information online about Africa that one would expect from a digital sphere dominated by Western concerns. According to Wikipedia, Africa is the world's third largest market and the most culturally diverse continent, "and yet it has the lowest and least informed profile of any region on the Internet; moreover, what does appear is often selective, lacks context and reinforces outdated stereotypes."[23]

As Tabita Rezaire discusses in her video piece *Afro Cyber Resistance*, the Cape Town-based collective Chimurenga experienced "the controlling and geographically biased architecture of the internet...Engaged in cultural African history and theory, they tried multiple times to upload African content onto Wikipedia, so as to Africanize the world's most visited online encyclopaedia and fill the lack of information online about the continent."[24] Elvira Dyangani Ose notes that many of those proposed entries were rejected, some "because their relevance was not proved, others because the style or tone of those entries was too personal or not deemed appropriate to the world's most 'open' Internet platform."[25])

Founded in 2007 by nonprofit lettera27 and contemporary art platform Africa Center, WikiAfrica is a collaborative project aimed at generating content sourced from Africans for publication on Wikipedia. Acknowledging that Wikipedia's content restrictions are an accessibility issue, WikiAfrica conducts workshops and training, engages field experts, and deploys other initiatives (such as Wiki Loves Women, in collaboration with the Goethe-Institut) to facilitate and encourage the publication of accurate, respectful information about Africa onto Wikipedia. The project intends to exist in concert with efforts to increase African internet access, which in June 2016 consisted of around 340 million online users, or 28.7% of the population.[26]

---

23. Wikipedia contributors, "Wikipedia:WikiAfrica," Wikipedia.
24. Rezaire, "Afro Cyber Resistance: South african internet art," 188.
25. Dyangani Ose, "Poetics of the Infra-Ordinary" (lecture, OCA Norway, Oslo, March 14, 2012.
26. Miniwatts Marketing Group, *Internet Users in Africa* March 2017.

There is a long way to go, but the production of true information about Africa, sourced from real Africans navigating Wikipedia's oppressive informatic norms, is valuable groundwork for dispelling anti-African stereotypes and increasing online African representation. Since one dimension of reparations involves knowledge transfer and the violence of in/visibility, WikiAfrica is a good rebuttal to the potential replication of Hegelian antiblack fantasies of Africa.

Though the project is a collaboration between a nonprofit and a contemporary art platform, it is not necessarily art, shirking aesthetic concerns to focus on the project of Africanizing Wikipedia and increasing digital literacy. As Rezaire states: "even if this endeavour is not thought of or seen as Internet Art per se, it can be understood as an online platform for active social resistance against occidental hegemony and online information control."[27] The art / non-art fluidity of WikiAfrica is not new to the African scene, and neither is its treatment of aesthetics as secondary to utility.

11.
BLACK RECLAMATION OF CRITICALITY

Reparations has a fiscal and resource access dimension as well as a representational dimension, but it also has a theoretical dimension. To stand against the supremacy of Western thought begins to lay the ground for the reclamation of critical aesthetics against European reason's history of Black dehumanization. Black feminist literary critic and theorist Hortense Spillers argues that the Black position is the critical position: "Because it was set aside,

---

27. Rezaire, "Afro Cyber Resistance: South african internet art," 188.

black culture could, by virtue of the very act of discrimination, become culture, insofar as, historically speaking, it was forced to turn its resources of spirit toward negation and critique."[28]

At a moment when criticality is so "in," Black criticality remains violently punished and pilfered. Its reclamation from assimilation to Western modalities becomes imperative. While complete non-assimilation to Western thought may be unavoidable due to the coloniality of the world, rejecting thought itself remains a possibility—*fuck thought, fuck that*—but it doesn't necessarily respond to the central problem.

what will communism do for
antiblackness pls will a bitch still
live in ontological death yes or no

Image courtesy of @delashereen.

---

28. Spillers, "The Idea of Black Culture," 28.

Instead, we might look deeper into the utility of thought itself, its use as a litmus for humanity to dehumanize Black and Brown people in service of conquest. The institution of thought represses the stark fact that dehumanized people, historically argued to lack reason, are in fact thinking humans. We can recalibrate the situation along the lines of Lewis Gordon: "Blackness… reaches out to theory, then, as theory split from itself. It is the dark side of theory, which, in the end, is none other than theory itself, understood as self-reflective, outside itself."[29]

Building on this, Jared Sexton argues that "1) all thought, insofar as it is genuine thinking, might best be conceived of as black thought and, consequently, 2) all researches, insofar as they are genuinely critical inquiries, aspire to black studies. Blackness is theory itself, anti-blackness the resistance to theory."[30] Just as the autonomous inutility of art remains impossible until the West repays its debt to Black and Brown aesthetics, so does a true *theory* detached from the sensory remain impossible until theory reconciles its antiblack dehumanizing uses.

Reclaiming criticality as properly Black may mean grappling with the possibility that, as Hortense Spillers argues, "black culture—as the reclamation of the critical edge…has yet to come."[31] If Black culture as reclamation of criticality's Blackness is a horizon, it remains clear that the intersection of Black assimilation to American imperialism and American genocide of Black people engen-

---

29. Gordon, "Theory in Black: Teleological Suspensions in Philosophy of Culture," 196.
30. Sexton, "Ante-Anti-Blackness: Afterthoughts."
31. Volcovici, "The Power Trip of the Black Exceptionalist in Space-Time."
32. James, "The Dead Zone: Stumbling at the Crossroads of Party Politics,

ders what Joy James calls a dead zone. "The nexus at which black achievement meets black genocide appears as a conceptual void."[32]

Art in a Larochean sense, as the conditional inclusion of Black artists to reify power and conceal modernism's debt to non-white aesthetics, is one such conceptual void. This prioritizes the necessity for action without a complete or cogent analytic, an imperative to redistribute resources now and ask questions later—or rather, an imperative to see such action as theory itself: repairing the schism between "thinking" and "thinking in black." James acknowledges the stumbling and illegibility involved in deploying an analytic from the dead zone: "The intersection is unlit...as we repeatedly cross our own past while projecting a real and imagined future as critical thought radically invents meaningful engagement."[33] While the reclamation of Black criticality remains but a horizon, we can look to projects like #PAYBLACK-TiME and WikiAfrica as examples of subversive engagement with the always already commoditized technics of sociality in order to repair the injustices and unequal access faced by Black artists around the world. In their fluid status and delegation of aesthetics to a utilitarian reparative role Black artists challenge the contemporary continuation of modernist violence, in line with a Black post-art to lay the groundwork for the reclamation of criticality's Blackness.

---

32. James, "The Dead Zone: Stumbling at the Crossroads of Party Politics, Genocide, and Postracial Racism," 460.
33. James, "The Dead Zone: Stumbling at the Crossroads of Party Politics, Genocide, and Postracial Racism," 476.

BIBLIOGRAPHY

abreu, manuel arturo. "Notes on the Garage Residency," *SFMoMa Open Space: Work on Work Blog*. September 14, 2016.

Descartes, Rene. *A Discourse on the Method of Correctly Conducting One's Reason and Seeking Truth in the Sciences*. Translated by Ian Maclean. New York: Oxford University Press, 2006.

Dyangani Ose, Elvira. "Poetics of the Infra-Ordinary." Lecture, OCA Norway, Oslo, March 14, 2012.

Gordon, Lewis. "Theory in Black: Teleological Suspensions in Philosophy of Culture," *Qui Parle: Critical Humanities and Social Sciences* 18.2 (2010): 192-214.

Hegel, GFW. *Hegel's Aesthetics: Lectures on Fine Arts, Vol 1*. Translated by T. M. Knox. Oxford: The Clarendon Press, 1975.

Hegel, GWF. *The Philosophy of History*. Kitchener, Ontario: Batoche Books, 2001.

James, Joy. "The Dead Zone: Stumbling at the Crossroads of Party Politics, Genocide, and Postracial Racism," *South Atlantic Quarterly* 108.3 (2009): 459-481.

Joselit, David. "Heritage and Debt." Lecture, Mack Lecture Series, Walker Art Center, Minneapolis , December 3, 2014. February 12, 2015.

Kaminsky, Jack. Hegel on Art: *An Interpretation of Hegel's Aesthetics*. New York: SUNY, 1962.

Kaprow, Allan Kaprow. *Essays on the Blurring of Art and Life*. Berkeley: University of California Press, 2003.

Laruelle, Francois. "The generic orientation of non-standard aesthetics." Lecture, Weisman Art Museum, Minneapolis, November 17, 2012. October 21, 2013.

Moten, Fred. *In the Break: The Aesthetics of the Black Radical Tradition*. Minneapolis: University of Minnesota Press, 2003.

Murrell, Denise. "African Influences in Modern Art." *The Met's Heilbrunn Timeline of Art History*. April 2008.

Negarestani, Reza. "The Labor of the Inhuman, Part II: The Inhuman." *e-flux Journal #53*. March 2014.

Obadike, Keith Townsend. "All Too Real The Tale of an On-Line Black Sale." Interview by Coco Fusco. Mendi + Keith Obadike. September 9, 2001.

Rezaire, Tabita. "Afro Cyber Resistance: South african internet art," *Technoetic Arts: A Journal of Speculative Research* 12.2 & 3 (2014): 185-196.

Sexton, Jared. Amalgamation Schemes: *Antiblackness and the Critique of Multiracialism*. Minneapolis: University of Minnesota Press, 2008.

Sexton, Jared. 2012. Ante-Anti-Blackness: Afterthoughts. *Lateral* 1. Cultural Studies Association.

Spillers, Hortense J. "The Idea of Black Culture," *CR: The New Centennial Review* 6.3 (2006): 7-28.

Volcovici, Geoffrey. "The Power Trip of the Black Exceptionalist in Space-Time." Black Quantum Futurism. January 1, 2017.

ONLINE IMAGINED BLACK ENGLISH

"Everybody want to be a nigga but nobody want to be a nigga."
—Paul Mooney as Negrodamus[1]

"Surely the net space just makes the same old burnt cork blackface routine easier."
—Keith Obadike[2]

1.
IMAGINED BLACK ENGLISH

The way people talk always changes, driven by language-internally or by social pressures. At any given moment in a language or dialect, certain aspects of speech are stable, and others are undergoing a change in progress. How does it happen? Who is responsible for it? How does the internet affect the process of language change?

I consider some of these questions for the case of Black English, the set of linguistic behaviors available to American members of the African diaspora. In recent decades, the advent of hip-hop and the internet have arguably spread Black media farther than ever before. As well, given that "Black English, especially the cadence, is becoming America's youth lingua franca, especially since the mainstreaming of hip-hop,"[3] I focus on the phenomenon of non-Black English speakers with no fluency using real or

---

[1]. Chappelle's Show Season 1, Episode 5. Aired 19 February 2003.
[2]. Fusco, C. 2001. All Too Real: The Tale of Black Sale: Coco Fusco interviews Keith Townsend Obadike. Thing Reviews.
[3]. Linguist John McWhorter quoted in Henderson, Nia-Malika. 2009. Blacks, whites hear Obama differently. Politico.com, 3 March 2009 (source).

imaginary linguistic features of Black English, which I call *imagined Black English*. This phenomenon is becoming more common because, as theorized by Cecilia Cutler, "hip-hop is increasingly claimed to be a multi-cultural lifestyle rather than a symbol of ethnic group identity, particularly by white adolescents, it seems to allow whites access to a commodified, ephemeral Black experience at various moments or phases in their lives without requiring overt claims of black ethnicity, and the sociolinguistic meaning of AAVE [African American Vernacular English] appears to be adjusted in the process."[4]

This phenomenon has been called borrowed Blackness,[5] Imagined African American Vernacular English,[6] linguistic appropriation,[7] mock Ebonics,[8] and linguistic minstrelsy,[9] the latter referring to one of the earliest American forms of this phenomenon in minstrel shows.[10] Many times these cross-racial language behav-

---

4. Cutler, Cecilia. 1999. Yorkville crossing: White teens, hip hop and African American English. Journal of Sociolinguistics 3: 435.
5. Bucholtz, M. 1999. You da man: Narrating the racial other in the production of white masculinity. Journal of Sociolinguistics 3: 443-460.
6. Chun, E. 2001. The construction of White, Black, and Korean American identities through African American Vernacular English. Journal of Linguistic Anthropology 11: 52-64.
7. Hill, J. 2011. The Everyday Language of White Racism. Oxford: Blackwell Publishing: 158; Reyes, Angela. 2005. Appropriation of African American slang by Asian American youth. Journal of Sociolinguistics 9.4: 509.
8. Ronkin, M. and Karn, H. 1999. Mock Ebonics: Linguistic racism in parodies of Ebonics on the internet. Journal of Sociolinguistics 3: 360-380.
9. Lopez, Q. 2009. Imitation or influence: White actors and Black language in film. Texas Linguistic Forum 53: 110–120; Bucholtz, M. and Lopez, Q. 2011. Performing blackness, forming whiteness: linguistic minstrelsy in Hollywood films. Journal of Sociolinguistics 15.5: 680–706.
10. See Mahar, W. 1985. Black English in early blackface minstrelsy: A new interpretation of the sources of minstrel show dialect. American Quarterly 37: 260– 285.

iors "do not correspond to most African Americans' linguistic patterns."[11] Often, Black language is borrowed and deracialized under the guise of being slang, even though slang is "a small set of new and usually short-lived words in the vocabulary of a dialect or language,"[12] while Black English is a fully-formed linguistic system, as all dialects and languages are. White supremacist society renders Blackness able to "travel on its own, separate and distinct from black people,"[13] globally marketed under systemic racism since ragtime sheet music, Black vaudeville, and race records to cultures across the world in the form of language, music, dance, and gesture. Of course, it has always been and "remains exceedingly attractive and possible in this post-black, post-soul age of black cultural traffic to love black cool and not love black people."[14]

At least since minstrelsy, non-Black Americans have borrowed from Black English and, more generally, Black culture for a variety of reasons, and the digital manifestation of this phenomenon is a part of this lineage. And at least since 1986's Jive Filter, linguistic minstrelsy has been an aspect of online talk, both in computer code, and in spontaneous speech.[15] Both spoken vernacular and internet vernacular are heavily indebted to Black English, "from everyday words… like tote or goober (peanut), to vernacular like

---

11. Bucholtz 1999: 445-446.
12. Rickford, R. 1999. African American Vernacular English. Malden: Blackwell Publishers, Inc: 321.
13. Elam, H. 2005. Change Clothes and Go: A Postscript to Postblackness. Black Cultural Traffic: Crossroads in Global Performance and Popular Culture (eds. H. Elam, Jr. and J. Kennell). Ann Arbor: The University of Michigan Press: 386.
14. Ibid.
15. The Jive Filter is the earliest in an antiblack tradition of "translator" computer programs, and is followed by examples such as De Ebonic Lectric Libary O De Classicks (1997), ebonics.irc (1999), Gizoogle (2005), englishtoghetto.com (2011), and others. This algorithmic heritage of digital minstrelsy is worth exploring further.

hip, cool, chill, dis or 24/7."[16] There is literally an app that only sends "yo" notifications.[17] The internet allows for communication and media dissemination to a wider and more diffuse audience than was once possible: individuals and communities with less and less relationship to Black media and linguistic behavior have access to it, with Urban Dictionary and Genius (formerly Rap Genius) only a few clicks away to provide "definitions." These conditions potentially alter or accelerate the process of deracialization by which words enter standard English, as well as provide more contexts for the performance of racist stereotypes. This whitewashing merits an analysis through the lens of language change, as well as a consideration of revising pre-internet models for the linguistic dimension of borrowed Blackness.

2.
CHANGING MODELS

Imagined Black English is an instance of code-switching, the "juxtaposition within the same speech exchange of passages of speech belonging to two different grammatical systems or subsystems."[18] Research on code-switching in computer-mediated communication tends to draw on frameworks developed for analyzing spoken, face-to-face discourse.[19] While online speech mirrors the debt to Black English evidenced by the spoken vernacular given

---

16. Young, K. 2012. The Grey Album: On the Blackness of Blackness. Minneapolis: Graywolf Press: 130.
17. Technically, you can currently actually attach links and location info to your "yos."
18. Gumperz, J. 1982. Discourse Strategies. Cambridge: Cambridge University Press: 59.
19. Androutsopoulos, Jannis. 2013. Code-switching in computer-mediated communication. Pragmatics of Computer-mediated Communication (eds. S. C. Herring, D. Stein & T. Virtanen) Berlin: de Gruyter Mouton: 667.

that "many of the practices of European American youth cultures, including linguistic practices, are borrowed from African American teenagers,"[20] face-to-face frameworks may be inadequate for many computer-mediated communication contexts.[21] Online talk is largely text-based, and may follow different sets of norms, particularly in more casual digital contexts such as chat.

Previous models[22] tended to categorize imagined Black English usage into (a) interpersonal contexts ranging from the vernacular to the institutional, and (b) mediatized contexts such as cinema and advertisement. While this may have been cogent in times when conversation and sociality themselves were not subsumed under capitalism, the corporatization of the internet throws this neat mediatized-non-mediatized distinction into question, since all online linguistic interaction serves as a potential profit venue for digital corporations. As such, pre-internet sociolinguistic models of imagined Black English may require revision to account for online imagined Black English. After all, we rightly decry desperate brands tweeting "bae" to remain relevant, but we never mention the fact that social media users posting about how their pumpkin spice latte is bae, or how their largely-White poetry reading was lit, are making these corporations money. This amounts to a denial of user agency, and requires correction.

While reasons for imagined Black English range from affinity to mockery to monetization, they generally follow the same pat-

---

20. Bucholtz, Mary. 2001. The whiteness of nerds: Superstandard English and racial markedness. Journal of Linguistic Anthropology, 11.1: 86.
21. Hinrichs, Lars. 2006. Codeswitching on the Web. Amsterdam: John Benjamins: 28-30.
22. See Bucholtz 1997, 1999; Cutler 1999; Hatala 1976; Labov 1980; Sweetland 2002.

tern: by "reshaping the meaning of the borrowed material into forms that advance their own interest," borrowers make the material "useless or irrelevant, or even antithetical, to the interests of the donor community." Stripped of its original context, "this reshaped meaning may then be imposed on donor speakers,"[23] which can be seen in instances such as Katy Steinmetz's 12 November 2014 New York Times article listing the Black English words "basic," "bae," "turnt," and "yasssss" among "words to ban in 2015."[24] This came on the heels of her 23 July 2014 article "This is What "Bae" Means."[25] Deracialized and decontextualized, these redefined words entered the mainstream lexicon at an accelerated rate due to the internet, and their proliferation among White Standard English speakers prompts exhaustion. Robin Boylorn corroborates this general tendency in her 14 January 2015 Guardian article called "Now that white people have declared 'bae' over, black people can use it in peace."

Further, uses of imagined Black English have always drawn their indexical meanings from the broader systemic context that makes this borrowing possible, since the time of "the genesis of the vernacular," which originated in the slaveholding South.[26] "As a consequence of racism, black masculinity in the United States has long been ideologically associated with a hyperphysicality that involves physical strength, hyper(hetero)sexuality, and physical violence."[27] In the afterlife of slavery, America reifies a set of stereotypes about Blackness—anger, creativity, negativ-

---

23. Hill 2011: 158.
24. Steinmetz, K. 2014. Which Word Should Be Banned in 2015? Time (source).
25. Steinmetz, K. 2014. This is What "Bae" Means. Time (source).
26. Rickford 1999: 324.
27. Bucholtz 1999: 444.

ity, stupidity, criminality, poverty, hypersexuality, and others—with which it justifies its denial of already-promised reparations, its continued murder and imprisonment of Black Americans, its ongoing redlining and gentrification policies after the Great Migration, and other antiblack national projects. As such, from the perspective of this larger context, imagined Black English is but one facet of systemic racism. After all, it is the "cultural elite and their allies who help enforce acceptable codes of linguistic conduct,"[28] using their power to decide the meanings and acceptable contexts of words.

Despite the fact that online imagined Black English largely draws its meanings from the same indexical pool as previous instances of borrowed Blackness, it may nevertheless involve novel linguistic behavior. Thus, is online imagined Black English a linguistic change in progress from pre-internet imagined Black English? In order to consider this question, it's necessary to first characterize language change in its relation to conscious intention, as well as what William Labov calls the gender paradox.

3.
DOES THE GENDER PARADOX OPERATE ONLINE?

Upwardly-mobile women are the leaders of linguistic change, but are also more likely to adopt standard speech behaviors. William Labov, one of the founders of sociolinguistics, calls this the "gender paradox." Labov identifies two kinds of language change:

---

[28]. Zeigler, M. and Osinubi, V. 2002. Theorizing the Postcoloniality of African American English. Journal of Black Studies 32.5: 588.

change from above the level of consciousness, and change from below the level of consciousness.[29] This dichotomy corresponds to the split between formal speech and vernacular speech. Change from above tends to begin in formal speech, spreading from upper to lower classes as the latter consciously adopt prestige linguistic forms. On the other hand, change from below primarily begins unconsciously in the vernacular talk of the working and lower-middle class, spreading to upper classes if it becomes more standard or sheds any stigma it might have.

While Labov argues that one of the characteristics of language change, especially from below, is its sporadic character,[30] in his search for innovators and leaders of linguistic change, he identifies these leaders as "women who have achieved a respected social and economic position in the local networks. As adolescents, they aligned themselves with the social groups and symbols that resisted adult authority, particularly when it was perceived as unfairly or unjustly administered, without deviating from their upwardly mobile path within the local social structure."[31] This alignment with alterity without any loss in social standing results in leaders of linguistic change having wide social networks from which to draw innovation into their own communities. This linguistic transfer is possible given that "if a certain group of speakers uses a particular variant then the social values attributed to that group will be transferred to that linguistic variant."[32] These

---

29. Labov, W. 2007. Transmission and Diffusion. Language 83.2: 348.
30. Labov, W. 2001. Principles of Linguistic Change, Vol. 2: Social Factors. Malden, MA: Blackwell Publishing: 75.
31. Ibid, 409.
32. Labov, W 1972. Sociolinguistic Patterns. Philadelphia: University of Pennsylvania Press: 25.

speakers adopt a "Janus-like"[33] role in the ways their contact with marginalized cultures make them a beacon for its entry into White culture without any reciprocity.

However, these upwardly-mobile young adult leaders of linguistic change exhibit behavior which Labov calls the "gender paradox." He argues from his data that women "show a lower rate of stigmatized variants and a higher rate of prestige variants than men"[34] and "adopt prestige forms at higher rates than men."[35] When a change is stable, he claims women tend to prefer prestige forms, whereas when a change from below is in progress, "women use higher frequencies of innovative forms than men do."[36] Thus, Labov characterizes the gender paradox as follows: "Women conform more closely than men to sociolinguistic norms that are overtly prescribed, but conform less than men when they are not."[37]

A standard network-theoretic explanation of the gender paradox is as follows: men's networks are more densely clustered and local, regional, nonstandard, and resistant to change; women's networks, on the other hand, tend to be more open and less local, leading to more access to innovative forms as well as a greater tendency to adopt non-regional standard variants.[38]

---

33. Hewitt, Roger. 1986. White talk Black talk: Inter-racial friendship and communication among adolescents. Cambridge and New York: Cambridge University Press: 144.
34. Labov 2001: 266.
35. Ibid, 272.
36. Ibid, 292.
37. Ibid, 293.
38. Romaine, S. 2003. Variation in Language and Gender. The Handbook of Language and Gender (eds. Holmes, J. and Meyerhoff, M). Maiden, MA and Oxford: Blackwell Publishing: 98-118.

Does the gender paradox operate online? Labov's notions of "local networks" may change in light of the internet; and the accelerated global dissemination of media may also mean a broader set of subversive groups and symbols from which to choose in the articulation and performance of identity, as well as a potentially wider social group in general. In their first report on global internet access, the United Nations' Broadband Commission Working Group reported in 2013 that only 2% fewer women than men were online in developed countries like the United States. Given that Labov's generalizations rely mostly on data collected from women living in developed countries, the relatively small size of the broadband gender gap for such nations entails the possibility of women being leaders of online language change.

As such, if online imagined Black English is a change in progress from below, Labov's argument would entail that non-Black women are its leaders. On the other hand, if online imagined Black English is a stable linguistic style variation, then whether non-Black women prefer or don't prefer it depends on the prestige of the particular feature, as well as whether the prescriptive sociolinguistic norms of its use are overt or covert. Truly answering this question would require quantitative data and is thus beyond the scope of this paper, but its theoretical import is worth considering. To do so, it's necessary to analyze the contextual prestige of Black English and the body of covert and overt norms surrounding its use.

4.
NORMS AND THE CONTEXTUAL PRESTIGE OF BLACK ENGLISH

While Black English is "America's youth lingua franca,"[39] the fact remains that "youths of all races and ages… often echo the negative attitudes of their parents, teachers, and the media toward AAVE [African American Vernacular English] and their positive attitude toward SAE [Standard American English.]"[40] And despite its true linguistic conservatism—"ax" is the older form of "ask,"[41] and habitual "be" can be traced to Hibernian English—Black English is often stigmatized as a sign of low intelligence,[42] to the extent that it is often not considered language.[43] This is an example of linguistic subordination, in which linguistic behavior associated with oppressed groups is viewed as linguistically deficient.[44] (Indeed, this tendency toward monolithic characterization exists even within sociolinguistics, with scholars commonly claiming that Black English has no regional variation.)[45]

---

39. Linguist John McWhorter quoted in Henderson, Nia-Malika. 2009. Blacks, whites hear Obama differently. Politico.com, 3 March 2009 (source).
40. Rickford 1999: 284.
41. Old English "acsian" -> Middle English "axe" -> Modern English "ask." E.g., from the 1535 Coverdale Bible, the text's first complete English translation: "Axe, and it shalbe geuen you: Seke, and ye shall fynde: knocke, and it shalbe opened vnto you." Matthew 7:7.
42. Ronkin and Karn 1999.
43. Ibid.
44. Lippi-Green, R. 1997. English with an accent: Language, ideology, and discrimination in the United States. London & New York: Routledge.
45. For discussion of regional variation of Black English, see Hinton, L. N., and Pollock, K. E. 2000. Regional Variations in the Phonological Characteristics of African American Vernacular English. World Englishes 19.1:59-71 and Thomas, E. R. 2007. Phonological and Phonetic Characteristics of AAVE. Language and Linguistics Compass: 450-475.

Therefore, there is a twoness at play in white America's treatment of Black English: it is "cool" currency in youth culture, but it is also bad English. By and large, the use norms are covert, especially in casual contexts. The Linguistic Society of America states that characterizations of Black English as "'slang,' 'mutant,' 'lazy,' 'defective,' 'ungrammatical,' or 'broken English' are incorrect and demeaning."[46] This is true, since, like any other dialect or language, Black English is governed by systematic morphosyntactic and phonological rules. While some may argue that the denigration of Black English is based on individual prejudice, "accent and dialect discrimination in hiring and firing have been tolerated by US courts,"[47] and the stigma Black English carries, as well as the dynamics of borrowed Blackness, are facets of systemic antiblackness. Language attitude research shows that this denigration takes on two dimensions: Black English scores low on status-related associations like education and wealth, but scores well on attractiveness-related associations like warmth.[48] Other studies, however, show low scores in these attractiveness categories as well.[49]

The vitriolic controversy surrounding the 1996 ebonics resolution exemplifies the association of Black English with low status in this set of linguistic ideologies. In the resolution, the Oakland Unified School District recognized Black English as a systematic form of language whose origins are African, as well as recogniz-

---

[46]. Resolution On The Oakland "Ebonics" Issue Unanimously Adopted at the Annual Meeting of the Linguistic Society of America, 1997.
[47]. Rickford 1999: 302.
[48]. See Buck 1968; Irwin 1977; Johnson & Buttny 1982; Garner & Rubin 1986; Speicher & Mahan 1992.
[49]. See Bishop 1979; Larimer et al 1988; Doss & Gross 1992, 1994; White et al 1998.

ing that "teachers often have unjustifiably negative attitudes towards students who speak AAVE [African American Vernacular English]" which "may lead them to have low expectations of such students... and to otherwise stunt their academic performance."[50] Students who cannot code-switch between standard English and Black English are at a disadvantage, because non-standard language behaviors among students negatively affect teachers' attitudes toward students. As such, the Oakland district instated a policy where pedagogy takes into account the disadvantages students face when their primary language is not standard English.[51] Essentially, teachers were to approach their lessons for these students as though they were teaching standard English as a second language. The following ad by The National Head Start Association, published in the 9 October 1998 issue of the New York Times, exemplifies the negative response to the resolution.[52]

---

50. Ibid: 283. A 1973 survey of 422 American teachers of various races also found that 40% held negative attitudes towards Black English, 40% held positive opinions, and 20% were ambivalent. Taylor, O. 1973. A survey of bidialectal language arts programs in the United States. Journal of Negro Education 52: 35-35.
51. Precedent for this case includes a successful 1977 court case in which Black working-class mothers whose children attended the Martin Luther King Junior Elementary School sued the Ann Arbor, MI school district, arguing that their children should be educated the same way as other students.
52. The poster reads: "Does this bother you? It should. We've spent over 400 years fighting for the right to have a voice. Is this how we'll use it? More importantly, is this how we'll teach our children to use it? If we expect more of them, we must not throw our hands in the air and agree with those who say our children cannot be taught. By now, you've probably heard about Ebonics (aka black [sic] English). And if you think it's become a controversy because white America doesn't want us messing with their precious language, don't. White America couldn't care less what we do to segregate ourselves. The fact is language is power. And we can't take that power away from our children with Ebonics. Would Dr. Martin Luther King, Malcolm X, and all the others who paid the price of obtaining our voice with the currency of their lives embrace this? If you haven't used your voice lately, consider this an invitation."

While it is true that much of the public outrage was due to media misinterpretation of linguistic terms like "genetic" in the resolution, as well as unclear language caused by the lack of a linguistic advisor in the resolution writing process, those who spoke out against the Oakland Unified School District's decision made their linguistic ideology clear: Black English is bad English, and educational contexts are no place for it. Indeed, the Oakland case brought the term "ebonics" to mainstream prominence.[53] "Ebonics" came to signify in the White American imaginary all of the negative stereotypes it imposes on Black language. Consider the top Google Image Search results for the term:

---

[53]. Williams, R. 1975. Ebonics: The True Language of Black Folks. St. Louis, MO: Institute of Black Studies.

But what are the attitudes towards Black English outside of such institutional contexts as school, work, and courts? Despite the covert stigma against Black English, characterized as defective English, in these "standard" contexts, Black English still continues to enter into the mainstream vernacular. However, when Black English terms enter "the lexicon, it is strange how suddenly their origins are not only declared unknown by the dictionary, but seemingly unknowable."[54] Linguist John McWhorter claims that Black English "conveys warmth, authenticity, and a touch of seductive danger."[55] These indexical meanings take on different significance based on who is speaking, as well as on context: for example, in institutional contexts, Black English faces heavy stigma, while in other contexts, this warmth, authenticity, and seductive danger may be communicative and pragmatic boons. In this sense, the same stereotyped indexical meanings that White supremacist culture imposes on Black English endow it with covert prestige in non-institutional contexts.

5.
BLACKNESS FOR SALE

To delineate these contextual valences of prestige and stigma, it is instructive to consider Keith Obadike's digital artwork *Blackness for Sale* (2001).[56] Drawn to explore the coloniality of digital language, in which "browsers called Explorer and Navigator... take you to explore the Amazon or trade in the eBay,"[57] Obadike

---

54. Young 2012: 130.
55. Linguist John McWhorter quoted in Henderson, Nia-Malika. 2009. Blacks, whites hear Obama differently. Politico.com, 3 March 2009 (source).
56. See ebay item Keith Obadike's Blackness.
57. Fusco, 2001.

takes to the latter to auction off his Blackness (the item acquired 12 bids and peaked at $152.50 until eBay shut it down after four days). This work exemplifies Harry Elam's notion that Blackness is able to "travel on its own, separate and distinct from black people"[58] as a commodity. Obadike's product description outlines the benefits that purchasing Blackness brings in certain contexts, while also warning against its use in other contexts. While this piece deals with Blackness in global capitalism more generally, its claims apply with respect to Black English. I quote the description in its entirety below, using Martine Syms' line breaks[59]:

> This heirloom has been in the possession of the seller for twenty-eight years. Mr. Obadike's Blackness has been used primarily in the United States and its functionality outside of the US cannot be guaranteed. Buyer will receive a certificate of authenticity.

Benefits and Warnings

Benefits:

1. This Blackness may be used for creating black art.

2. This Blackness may be used for writing critical essays or scholarship about other blacks.

---

[58]. Elam 2005: 386.
[59]. Syms, M. 2013. Black Vernacular: Reading New Media. Presented at SXSW Interactive 2013.

3. This Blackness may be used for making jokes about black people and/or laughing at black humor comfortably. (Option#3 may overlap with option#2)

4. This Blackness may be used for accessing some affirmative action benefits. (Limited time offer. May already be prohibited in some areas.)

5. This Blackness may be used for dating a black person without fear of public scrutiny.

6. This Blackness may be used for gaining access to exclusive, "high risk" neighborhoods.

7. This Blackness may be used for securing the right to use the terms "sista," "brotha," or "nigga" in reference to black people. (Be sure to have certificate of authenticity on hand when using option 7).

8. This Blackness may be used for instilling fear.

9. This Blackness may be used to augment the blackness of those already black, especially for purposes of playing "blacker-than-thou."

10. This Blackness may be used by blacks as a spare (in case your original Blackness is whupped off you.)

Warnings:

1. The Seller does not recommend that this Blackness be used during legal proceedings of any sort.

2. The Seller does not recommend that this Blackness be used while seeking employment.

3. The Seller does not recommend that this Blackness be used in the process of making or selling "serious" art.

4. The Seller does not recommend that this Blackness be used while shopping or writing a personal check.

5. The Seller does not recommend that this Blackness be used while making intellectual claims.

6. The Seller does not recommend that this Blackness be used while voting in the United States or Florida.

7. The Seller does not recommend that this Blackness be used while demanding fairness.

8. The Seller does not recommend that this Blackness be used while demanding.

9. The Seller does not recommend that this Blackness be used in Hollywood.

10. The Seller does not recommend that this Blackness be used by whites looking for a wild weekend.

Obadike's list of warnings is meant to clarify how existing consumer and linguistic commodities that index Blackness work: they do not burden the buyer or speaker with the drawbacks of Blackness, but instead draw a phantasmagoric aura from them in a way that justifies antiblack structural racism, as well as overdetermines Blackness, rendering it a flat vector of cool, seductive danger that is tolerated for entertainment purposes and is otherwise eliminated by a militarized police state and its deputized settler citizens. This aligns with the racist overdetermination of Blackness that has been occurring since minstrelsy times, when Black performers had to don burnt cork blackface to "correctly" indicate the Blackness that occupied the white imaginary. Obadike argues that "to many white artists, blackness represents some kind of borderless excess, some kind of unchecked expression."[60] The history of borrowed Blackness, from minstrelsy to Mailer's postwar White negro to the wigger and beyond, operates exactly within the affective landscape Obadike identifies. However, language change is an ecology, not a monolith, and the influence that upwardly-mobile women leaders of linguistic change exert is determined on a community-by-community basis. It's instructive to look at a number of examples in the case of online imagined Black English.

6.
GENDERED ECOLOGIES OF DIGITAL MINSTRELSY

Online social networks tend to pattern similarly to meatspace ones,[61] entailing that generally speaking, upwardly-mobile White women are leaders of digital linguistic change. In the case of online imagined Black English, this is true for terms like "on fleek," which entered the white mainstream via Ariana Grande's MTV rendition of Peaches Monroe,[62] or "Netflix and chill."[63] However, a more finely-grained view may show that this is not the case in every online linguistic community of practice, revealing a gendered ecology of borrowed Blackness where upwardly-mobile women play different roles in different spaces, and borrowing takes on various entextualized styles based on information format. It is reasonable to assume that online spaces with fewer

---

60. Fusco 2011.
61. Pérez-Sabater, C. 2012. The Linguistics of Social Networking: A Study of Writing Conventions on Facebook. Linguistik online 56.2.
62. See Ariana Grande's Vine.
63. See Brittany Furlan's Vine, as well as Kevin Roose's timeline for "Netflix and chill" at Fusion.

would-be leaders of linguistic change, or which are unwelcoming to them, reflect their influence less than other spaces. But because content can travel from one online community of practice to another, it is not necessarily the case that male-dominated spaces prevent upwardly-mobile women from being leaders of online linguistic change. Instead, denser, more localized and nonstandard male-dominated communities exist at a different point in the structure than do less local, more standard, change-receptive women communities. The network structure aids the deracialization of the content as it moves toward the digital mainstream and away from "lawless," anonymized areas of the internet.

Reddit, the self-described "front page of the internet," is dominated by men.[64] Unlike, say, Pinterest, whose user base is predominantly White women,[65] it is likely that much of the linguistic innovation on reddit is due to men. The racism of some corners of reddit deserves its own essay; the short version is that reddit has been sort of trying to clean up its act since 2013. With respect to online imagined Black English, the subreddit r/BlackPeopleTwitter operates as a means of surveillance of Black culture and language, engendering a situation analogous to "white male bonding through Black music,"[66] except with digital content operating as the relational platform. Unlike racist subreddits like r/niggers, banned in 2013, r/BlackpeopleTwitter has explicit rules against

---

64. Duggan, M and Smith, A. 2013. 6% of Online Adults are reddit Users. Pew Research Center, Washington, D.C.
65. Duggan, M., Ellison, N., Lampe, C., et al. 2015. Demographics of Key Social Networking Platforms. Pew Research Center, Washington, D.C.; Krogstad, J.M. 2015. Social media preferences vary by race and ethnicity. Pew Research Center, Washington, D.C.
66. Keil, C. and Feld, S. 1994. Music Grooves: Essays and Dialogues. Chicago: The University of Chicago Press: 2.

racism and doxxing. Presumably, the subreddit's users surveil Twitter for content due to its demographics: 28% of Twitter users are Black, while 20% of its users are white.[67] But the surveillance of Black Twitter is not specific to reddit. Black Twitter has long been a source of material for those engaging in borrowed Blackness. Further, the monitoring and monolithic characterization of "Black Twitter" has gone on at least since Choire Sicha's 2009 article[68] as well as Farhad Manjoo's 2010 Slate article, "How Black People Use Twitter,"[69] with its infamous "Twitter bird of color," pictured here.

Stats
Page impressions per month: 680,000,000
Unique visitors per month: 22,000,000
Posts per day: 1,000,000
Alexa Traffic Rank: 800 (Global) & 401 (US)
Google PageRank: 6

Demographic
Age: 18-34
Gender: ~70% male, ~30% female
Location: United States (47%), United Kingdom (8%), Canada (6%), Australia (5%), Germany (4%), France (2%), Sweden (2%), Netherlands (2%), Poland (1.5%), Brazil (1.5%)
Interests: Japanese culture, anime, manga, video games, comics, technology, music, movies
Education: Majority attended or currently enrolled in college

---

67. Duggan, M., Ellison, N., Lampe, C., et al. 2015.
68. "What Were Black People Talking About on Twitter Last Night?"
69. "How Black People Use Twitter." Slate.

Demographic data are harder to use in constructing a framework for racialization on sites who keep such information private. For example, 4chan, Cracked, BuzzFeed, and other sites have requested that Quantcast not reveal their demographic data. 4Chan, however, self-reports its demographics (pictured here), and like reddit, it is male-dominated.[70] 4chan is a particularly intense site of content creation activity, described by the Washington Post as "the original incubator for a huge number of memes and behaviors we now consider central to mainstream Internet culture."[71] Engineered or otherwise, 4chan's cultural influence is enormous—its founder, moot, was Time's Most Influential Person of 2009 thanks to users manipulating the poll. However, 4chan is not only largely populated by men according to its own reports; it is not welcoming to women. 2014's Fappening, in which 4chan users leaked hundreds of nude photos of largely women celebrities, sealed the deal on this, but it had been clear at least since 2006, around the time the phrase "Tits or GTFO" began becoming popular on 4chan.

Further, due to its anarchic anonymity, 4chan has long had a history of being a repository for virulent racism. Indeed, in 2010 the "Racists on 4chan" meme rose to popularity. It characterized the "drastic discrepancies between how a typical bigot interacts with minorities in real-life"[72] versus on the internet. While it mocks these white bigots who spout slurs online, the meme itself is racist, made by the very same kind of person: it depicts the Black man as a silhouette with minstrel-like bright red lips, and the meme's original name was "niggerwalk"[73]:

---

70. See: http://www.4chan.org/advertise.
71. Dewey, C. 2014. Absolutely everything you need to know to understand 4chan, the Internet's own bogeyman. The Washington Post.
72. http://knowyourmeme.com/memes/racists-on-4chan.
73. Ibid.

And in June 2010, 4chan users manipulated Google Trends so that the n-word topped the list[74]:

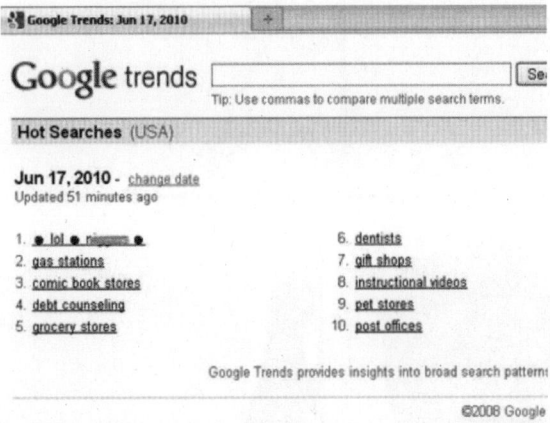

If 4chan is indeed at the center of innovation in internet culture, with its influence spreading outward toward the mainstream, then it is reasonable to argue that its violent antiblack racism also filters outward and informs the mainstream toolkit available for the performance of digital minstrelsy, however subtle or flagrant. Therefore, while would-be leaders of linguistic change do not seem welcome on 4chan and other male-dominated sites, as these sites' activity crosses thresholds to other sites and social networks to become more palatable, a version of the content eventually reaches these upwardly-mobile women. A potential example of this process is the recently-popular #RealNiggaHours meme.

---

74. Franzen, C. 2010. Google Trends Hacked With Racial Slur (Again!). Politics Daily.

7.
#REALNIGGAHOURS

The earliest online mentions of the phrase "real nigga hours" are:

1. a 13 Oct 2009 tweet by MrBMB at 3:51am that reads "Real Nigga hours who upp?"[75]

2. a Facebook page launched on 8 April 2011, titled "Real Nigga Hours From 1am-5am Check In #103."[76]

The phrase denotes the late-night hustle, which is an old idea in rap—e.g., Nas said in 1994 that sleep is the cousin of death. While "nigga" generally indexes a Black speaker,[77] the phrase recently caught on among non-Black internet users, seemingly trafficking in an old stereotype that much Black social media activity, such as Black Twitter, occurred late at night. It began to gain traction thanks to two popular Facebook groups which post memes featuring variations of the phrase and concept: "Niggaz Still WILIN," created on 25 April 2014, and "Real Nigga Hours Who Up," launched on 18 August 2014. Among other kinds of content, these two groups post overcompressed, Steyerlian "poor images" styled after Black digital content to index masculinity through Blackness. The images generally marry the trope of late night internet use with the injunction to "smash that like," a phrase which likely originated in online video game communities around 2012.[78]

---

75. https://twitter.com/MrBMB/status/4830333176.
76. https://www.facebook.com/pages/Real-Nigga-Hours-From-1am-5am-Check-In-103.
77. Spears, A. 1998. African-American language use: Ideology and so-called obscenity. African-American English (eds. S. Mufwene, J. Rickford, G. Bailey, and J. Baugh). London: Routledge: 226-250.
78. See: http://knowyourmeme.com/memes/smash-the-like.

These two groups emerged in the wake of Urban Dictionary user Joselaw submitting an entry for the phrase:

real nigga hours

The time in the day between 2:30 a.m. and 5 a.m.

What time is it Josie? Its real nigga hours

by Joselaw February 27, 2014

A typical #RealNiggaHours image looks like the following:

The phrase eventually reached the BlackPeopleTwitter subreddit, and as such a more mainstream white gaze, with Redditor Ahseyo submitting the following image macro on 25 September 2015[79]:

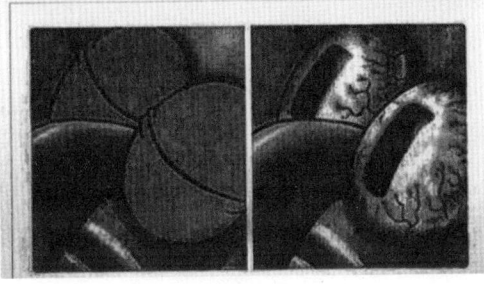

Five days later, Ryder Ripps, a White net artist, posted the article "11 Wild Reasons Why #RealNiggaHours Is The Greatest Meme Of All Time" to Medium, around the same time the "#RealNiggaHours" KnowYourMeme page was created. In his Medium article, Ripps engages in the standard pattern of "reshaping the meaning of the borrowed material into forms that advance [his] own interest," to make the borrowed material "useless or irrelevant, or even antithetical, to the interests of the donor community."[80] He is aware that #RealNiggaHours "can be interpreted as offensive, especially when its purveyors are white. It can be interpreted as making fun of meme formats that are prevalent within the black

---

[79]. See: https://www.reddit.com/r/BlackPeopleTwitter/comments/3mc6dr/real_nigga_hours/.
[80]. Hill 2011: 158.

[sic] community."[81] However, he instead sees it as "illuminating truths about shared internet experience, and not a thing about race."[82] Note well the antiblack mental gymnastics at work here: the use of a slur is meant to bring (White?) people together with respect to time, "the ultimate shared experience."

For Ripps, the meme's use of the slur is also about freedom. His tenth reason for #RealNiggaHours being the greatest meme of all time is that it "represents pure freedom," which echoes Obadike's claim that "to many white artists, blackness represents some kind of borderless excess, some kind of unchecked expression."[83] This holds across history: it is as true for dada sound poets who claimed "that their nonsensical utterances were based on the sounds that Negroes make"[84] as it is for White male meme makers. The threat of mainstream muzzling, which Ripps seems to imply has happened to memes such as doge, lolcats, and others, is not present to stunt this freedom. For Ripps, #RealNiggaHours is "wayyyyy to[o] abstract and edgy for normies to get. #RealNiggaHours is truly for real ones only, you WILL NOT FIND this meme in Urban Outfitters campaigns." I think the implication here is that Ripps fancies himself a real nigga (or "real one" as he says) because he sometimes stays up late online, and makes memes using or referencing antiblack slurs.

Ripps is correct that a meme format with a slur will probably not catch on in the mainstream. However, recall what was stated earlier: as content styles "surface upward" from less mainstream

---

81. Ripps, R. 2015. 11 Wild Reasons Why #RealNiggaHours Is The Greatest Meme Of All Time. Medium.com.
82. Ibid.
83. Fusco 2011.
84. Ibid. See for example Huelsenbeck's chants negres, or Picabia's

sites to more mainstream ones, the content becomes more palatable—that is to say, deracialized. Ripps seems to be unaware of his own role in this mainstreaming process: he aligns himself with the "Real ones" despite arriving late to the meme, arguing that it's "not a meme people who aren't HEAVY users will understand." Given the accelerated nature of media dissemination, this process has arguably already happened with #RealNiggaHours, evidenced by the following image posted to /r/CrappyDesign with no mention of racialized origins on 6 October 2015:

In this case, reddit may be analyzed as a sort of threshold between the "deeper corners" of the internet which are unwelcome to leaders of linguistic change, such as 4chan, and the digital mainstream. Of course, in order to formulate a more thorough analysis of how different gendered online communities of practice interact, and how this network structure plays into both the process of deracialization and antiblack iconicity, I would require quantitative data. I hope to have provided a theoretical sketch in this paper for future researchers to pursue data collection, in order to more fully characterize the relationship between IRL and URL borrowed Blackness.

In the 19th century, minstrel shows seem to have emerged among white American men as a response to a fomenting abolitionist movement and increasing job competition from free Blacks. Descendants of this lineage are far and wide, such as John Berryman's Henry in the 77 Dream Songs, which won a Pulitzer in the Civil Rights Era for a portrayal of Americanness that included Henry's minstrel sidekick Sir Bones. While Katherine Davis argues that "Berryman made it clear that he meant the [minstrel] dialect to express himself as 'imaginary Negro' . . . going beyond mere sympathy to an imaginative identification with oppressed peoples,"[85] this act is clearly part of a long lineage of minstrelsy that draws on negative stereotypes of American Blackness in the construction of white identity, and in this case a white aesthetic. In light of this historical context, the case of hip-hop's global and digital dominance in a time of #BlackLivesMatter presents a new example in which political turmoil results in a response from whites and other non-Blacks involving borrowed Blackness. As Obadike puts it, "surely the net space just makes the same old burnt cork blackface routine easier."[86]

---

85. Davis, K. 1985. "Honey Dusk Do Sprawl": Does Black Minstrel Dialect Obscure The Dream Songs? Language and Style 18.1: 33-34.
86. Fusco 2011.

TRANSTRENDER: A MEDITATION ON GENDER AS A RACIAL CONSTRUCT

"It would be better to disclose the confinement rather than make illusions of freedom."
—Robert Smithson

"Glissant says the Middle Passage made it possible 'to consent not to be a single being.' What does it mean to have been sent to give yourself away? Pretty much everybody I know is driven to dissent from such a movement, where consent is inseparable from a monstrous imposition..."
—Fred Moten

1.
THE NEW DIGITALITY

The corporatization of the internet brought about the demise of what Nathan Jurgenson calls digital dualism—the belief in "online" and "offline" as separate spaces. The appified digital strip mall we call the internet today presents itself as simply another aspect of reality, and bears little resemblance to the badly-coded badlands of two or three decades prior, populated by anonymous avatars seeking virtual solace from meatspace.

This digital, fluid terrain proved critical for many nascent trans people, including me. But the "URL/IRL" distinction collapsed in favor of a more temporal metaphor of digitality, as corporations gained control of the data stream, seeking to better track, manipulate, and monetize users. Facebook's recent name policy exemplifies this shift—whereas anonymous avatars once represented a site for trans people to reclaim, control, and extend their identities, now our digital footprint must align with the state's identification system in the wake of the Real ID Act of 2005 and the FBI's Activity-Based Intelligence paradigm, launched in 2010.

The ideology of Big Data requires that our actions be locatable to begin with: anchored to one specific quantified identity. If the multiplicity and fluidity of the early digital sandbox finds its beginnings in the Middle Passage, as Fred Moten paraphrases Edouard Glissant in my epigraph, then the demise of digital dualism may mirror and aid colonial capitalism's revocation of this possibility to consent not to be a single being. The tragedy of this formulation is that not being a single being has a double meaning: both more than one, and also not even one. I try to trace out this double meaning particularly in the context of race's presence in trans.

Along with the internet's gentrification, trans is trending. This is a symptom of the recent generalization of queerness as any marketable deviation from norm. This reifies legibility and aligns precisely with a militaristic Big Data surveillance paradigm in which "it is the unknown that becomes targeted," as Grégoire Chamayou puts it. Drawing somewhat morbid inspiration from Joe Biden's loaded statement that transgender discrimination is "the civil rights issue of our time," I trace the continuing presence and role of race in this nexus of contexts, in order to discuss the hegemonic histories, implications, and aspirations of queer and trans discourse in light of the new digitality. I ultimately argue that what seem like novel developments need to be considered in light of actually-existing diachronic and synchronic conditions, namely the conditions of race.

2.
TRANS IS TRENDING

We live in times where everything has been queered, but we are "not yet queer," as the late José Muñoz put it. Queerness is futurity itself, by this line of thought; or, by another, more thanatological line of thought such as that of the neo-Bersanists (Lee Edelman, Jack Halberstam, et al), queerness is the rejection of this futurity. In either formulation, a certain gentrification or generalization of queerness is present, what Jordana Rosenberg calls "queer atonality": any deviation from norm can be characterized as queer, and any norm can be claimed to have queer undercurrents trembling within it. The implicit problem here is one of legibility. Indeed, in Queer Ecology Timothy Morton writes that since "at the DNA level, it's impossible to tell a "genuine code sequence from a viral code insertion," it follows that "there is no contradiction between straightforward biology and queer theory."

For people who uphold the supremacy of medical evidence in delineating the definitions and goals of the LGBTQIA+ "community," as well as visible difference more generally, a statement like Morton's makes sense. For those who are skeptical of reifying science, the statement seems questionable: is biology straightforward? If Morton is repudiating a contradiction between biology and queer theory, what does this contradiction look like? What are the "genuine code sequences" that he argues cannot be distinguished from "viral code insertions"? What are the methods of distinguishing? Parallel to these questions, it also seems that this generalization of queerness as difference-of-whatever affects every subcommunity under the "queer" umbrella, including the trans community. The framework of trans has been generalized to various non-transgender, as well as non-western, groups: consider trans-ableist, trans-species (otherkin), and trans-ethnic communities and identities, as well as the symbolically "inclusive" use of the asterisk in the term "trans*."

In short, everything can be read as queer, which means nothing is queer. Trans is trending, which may or may not help, but most likely hurts, actually-existing trans people. A concrete institutional definition of trans is still "under construction," itself having undergone various "queerings." But both above and under the carnival of signifiers and the circulation of theoretical concepts, trans people, especially of color, still inordinately suffer and die. Our voices are still unheard and ignored, even as aspects of the condition become generalized and hypervisible. The world cheers on as we agonize. Statistics about trans people of color get subsumed into the general trans struggle to intensify empathy. What, precisely, is this necropolitics of conceptualization whereby trans pain, particularly the pain of black trans people, continues to transmute into metaphors, generalities, theoretical developments, queerings, coping mechanisms for people who think they were "born into the wrong race," and much more, but basic human rights and even expectancy of life itself still elude many in the global trans community? When did queerness become a post-critical theory clickbait machine?

In considering the cultural currency of our pain and death, it's instructive, if somewhat chilling, to follow Morton's argument from a racial perspective: if biology is queer by virtue of the paradox of categorizing norm deviation, then white society positions the racialized Other as its inherently queer counterpart. In its encounter with difference, white society then colonizes and categorizes, generally erroneously (such as, for example, according to genetic thresholds), in order to uphold violent regimes of visibility. Further, if we agree with Morton that distinguishing Self from Other, Genuine from Fake, or Life from Virus is difficult (even impossible), and we follow his assertion regarding "the difference multiplication that is queer theory's brilliance," then some analytic lines of flight begin to emerge: queer theory is like the randomness of mutation in nature, and aids the creation of categories of differentiation, which are not only useful for individual self-realization, but also distinguishing (impossibly, Morton might say) entities within a cultural ecology—that is to say, state data gathering, which has its roots in racial slavery.

Queerness qua entropy gentrifies into the rhizomatic expansion of census categories, the development of predatory tracking and marketing paradigms, and the financialized enclosure of affect: "if your gender isn't one of the 56 available on Facebook, is it real?" I follow some of these lines of thought throughout this essay in a suitably convoluted way. First, I consider the history of the relation between surveillance and race. Then, I discuss an ideological split regarding the definition of trans. I go on to discuss the transvaluation of trans by means of considering two examples of the gentrification of trans terminology: outside our community, trans-ethnic discourse; and within our community, the symbolic inclusivity politics of the asterisk (as in, "trans*"). The transvaluation of trans makes explicit the hegemonic implications and aspirations of western trans discourse.

Ser Serpas, *pay to cum (but didn't)*, 2017.
Site-specific fabric installation. Dimensions variable.
Courtesy the artist and Queer Thoughts gallery.

3.
SURVEILLANCE AND RACE

In his quip about queer theory and biology, Morton posits that the aleatory nature of the world's molecular level mirrors deconstruction's claim that no text is truly authentic. This, then, entails that there is no truly authentic life-form, and ecology has always already escaped governmentality. But this does not really reflect reality, since even if it's metaphysically true, in practice, societies are very much characterized by positing an authentic form, finding or inventing the Other, and either extracting life (slavery), purging this category (settler colonialism), or both (really-existing capitalist democracy).

The "age of the algorithm," as Luciana Parisi calls it, is simply the most recent manifestation of technologies for tracking and manipulating people. Digital anonymity, too, is only one recent instance of state agents being unable to tell "genuine code sequences" and "viral insertions" apart. The homogenized, dark-skinned enemy Other is the motivating force of the American empire itself, and arguably the beginning of American surveillance is the slave pass system—these slips of paper, in conjunction with the illegality of slave literacy, allowed whites to let their slaves off the plantations and be identifiable. But slaves, which whites often could not tell apart anyway, secretly learned English and consistently foiled this early surveillance tactic.

Presentation politics were more fluid when slave passes simply had names and short descriptions—slaves could impersonate others, pretend to be plantation locals, and employ other survivalist deceptions. But instances like the 1739 Stono Rebellion, the Haitian Revolution, and other slave revolts motivated property owners to develop more sophisticated tracking systems. For example, in 1783, Charleston adopted metal slave hire badges, some of America's earliest numbered IDs, meant for "payment of the annual slave tax" and ensuring "political control of black people as a class." (Christian Parenti, The Soft Cage: Surveillance in America from Slavery to the War on Terror, 2004). Another example: free papers that were impossible to forge without a printing press, and which contained elaborate biometric descriptions.

With the shift from plantation slavery to forced prison labor as the handmaiden to Fordism, as well as the introduction of other ethnic minorities into the American workforce, biometrics became a way of counteracting the white perception of racialized others as indistinguishable. The biometric tendency began in earnest in 1891, when Croatian-born Argentinian anthropologist and police official Juan Vucetich began expanding the ideas of eugenics inventor Francis Galton in order to develop dactyloscopy—fingerprinting. Harris Hawthorne Wilder stated in 1902 that dactyloscopy "would be of great service... in the official identification of Chinese, Negroes, and other races the features of which at least to the Caucasian eye, offer hardly sufficient individuality to be at all times trustworthy." The uniqueness of genetic code, then, served as a means for white America to better distinguish among a putative illegible, criminal horde.

In the production of normative bodies, the biometric impulse to distinguish among this horde can be contrasted with, and emerges from, the photochemical impulse against distinguishing. A good example of this is the history of Kodak's color reference cards, "shirley cards," which used white models. This meant the film did not reflect the diversity of darker skin tones. Godard refused to use Kodak film in 1977 for an assignment in Mozambique, arguing that the film stock was inherently racist.

That same year, Polaroid finally divested financial support from apartheid thanks to a seven-year campaign by the Polaroid Revolutionary Workers Movement. As such, consider Polaroid's solution to the Kodak conundrum (which went unsolved until Kodak introduced "multiracial" shirley cards in 1995). Polaroid's vintage ID-2 camera had a Boost button: it caused the flash to emit 42% more light in order to accommodate dark skin, which absorbs 30-40% more light than white skin. But is more exposure the solution to invisibility or indistinguishability?

I borrow "photochemical" from Fanon, who uses the term to describe the west's process of epidermalization whereby a manichean symbolism is grafted onto dark skin as though with a fixative. In this regime, light signifies knowing, the good, and the beautiful; dark signifies ignorance, the evil, and the ugly. Epidermalization thus both conditions both the biometric and photochemical urges of white supremacy. And yet, if the proposition of white supremacy is that dark skin signifies all this bad stuff, how does one know this, aside from the tautological negricide of a militarized police force on a search-and-destroy mission? What is the phenomenology here? A quote from Charles Johnson is instructive. Describing epidermalization in a 1993 essay, he writes: "All I am, can be to them is as nakedly presented as the genitals of a plant since they cannot see my other profiles. My subjectivity is turned inside out like a shirtcuff."

Following one potential reading of this quote, the manicheanism of epidermalization is libidinal. Whiteness is disembodied, theoretical; blackness is fleshy, visceral. This is because the unknowable, the criminal, and the bad as sites of encounter all have a sexual valence in America, whose Puritan veil conceals or represses a Wild West settler-colonial hedonism. The unknown is both reviled and explored—the site where knowledge is forged through the exteriorization of black subjectivity. But for the hegemon to do this, it must be able to locate (create) this signifier of the unknown. The reduction of the black to a genital or reproductive role is essential to capitalism's material, cultural, and conceptual expansion. Consider some examples: white male bonding through black music, as Steven Felds puts it; the role of black labor (whether in slavery or ostensible citizenship) in settler-colonial capitalism's efforts to disappear the native; and the experimental manipulation of low-income black bodies (the role of Henrietta Lacks in immortal cell line research, or of COINTELPRO as a pilot of the modern surveillance paradigm, et al).

Moreover, this framework, parasitic on the presence of dark skin as such, extends away from visibly-black people, as I consider later. The west's concept of black—as pain, crime, violence, the unknown—is what allows for the formulation of the regimes of visibility of normative gender presentation and identity, as well as the criminalization of "gender deception." This is revealed not only in the "tyranny of genitalia" and genitalized dysphoria, as well as in the trans discourse of passing, borrowed from race, but also in an ideological split both internal and external to the trans community regarding the status of medical evidence, dysphoria, performativity of trans, and even what trans is.

Rindon Johnson, *They are running together because they sink up together, it feels like they are running slower but they are actually running faster, they are running faster together*, 2018.
**Furniture Leather, Black Ebonizing Dye.
Courtesy the artist and AA|LA Gallery.**

4.
DEFINING TRANS

Capitalism's manichean racial nucleus and its tension between a biometric and photochemical impulse inform categories of visible gender difference. Such difference is an indelible, nonobjective category in all gendered societies—this visibility serves as the bedrock for defining normative gender. But how does race inform the conditions of possibility for this visibility, and for its legibility or lack thereof? Emerging "on paper" from the racialized medical-industrial complex, trans as category and discourse serves as a crucial fault line and vantage point for considering regimes of visibility and the policing of difference in racial capitalism.

Internal and external to the digital trans community, there exist two general tendencies for defining trans, both of which reify different performances of legibility: a medicalization orientation and an identitarian orientation. Both paradigms agree that the psychological pathologization of trans is harmful to our community. Briefly: the removal of homosexuality from the DSM co-occured with the introduction of gender dysphoria to its pages. By presenting dysphoria as purely psychological, the DSM entry allows for the argument that trans people don't need any more medical access than therapy. Thus, in spite of the split among the trans community, both paradigms agree on two things: that trans people, however defined, require medical access, and that trans is not a psychological disorder.

What is it, then? For the medicalization group, trans is a neurological condition. This group privileges medical evidence about brain structure above all else. Because there is no medical evidence of nonbinary brains, medicalizationists may often consider nonbinary, genderfluid, and genderqueer trans people, as well as trans people who don't experience dysphoria, "not really trans." The identitarians, on the other hand, see trans as an inherently political position with respect to categories of difference within capitalism, and privileges personal accounts about oppression above all else. The argument is that trans as political identity challenges capitalism's regime of binary gender assignment, its relegation of reproductive labor to the unwaged "feminine" sphere. Instead, as we've known since John Money's controversial work and his creation of the term "gender identity," there are more than two sexes, potentially infinite actual genders, and a multitude of invasive cross-cultural procedures for making people fit capitalism's two "genders."

As a Dominican nonbinary trans person of color not currently interested in transitioning, I don't see any particular advantage to either position. Medicalizationists have no room for me, since, as Toby Beauchamp puts it, medical "surveillance focuses first on individuals' legibility as transgender, and then, following medical interventions, on their ability to conceal any trans status or gender deviance." (Beauchamp 2009: 357). On the other hand, identitarians overdetermine my life circumstances, particularly my gender, as inherently political. Further, the politicization of dysphoria, "coming-out" narratives and queer-nationalist oppression olympics draw their pathological power from the subsumption of trans of color narratives: just as white "Men's Rights activists" leech off statistics about men of color to give import to their cause, the mainstream, whitewashed image of the suffering trans person gains much of its traction from sociological statistics about trans of color circumstances. However, from the vantage point of my dysphoria, I do find myself more drawn to the identitarian position. Medicalizationists are sometimes called "truscum" for advocating that you need dysphoria to be trans. Conversely, the term "transtrender" often denotes someone who identifies as trans and does not (ever or often) experience dysphoria.

An identitarian understanding of trans is more agnostic and fluid about dysphoria, and I'm drawn to this because I don't think hatred, disgust, fear, and other negative feelings about one's genitalia and gender role are trans-specific. Neither do I think that all trans people "should" feel these feelings and others characteristic of dysphoria. It would be bad science to argue that whatever neurological conditions result in trans also deterministically result in dysphoric feelings. However, I also find the identitarian focus on anticapitalist, "binary-smashing" performativity to be a metaphysical limit on what trans can be, as though our value as living people is entirely reducible to the metaphorical value of our circumstances in the struggle against capitalism. As such, both sides of the ideological divide are regimes of legibility originating in race, whether it's the reification of medical evidence and trans-exclusivity of dysphoria of one faction, or the emphasis on performativity, "identity-exploration," and "coming-out" stories of the other faction.

I want to ride this ideological divide in trans from the perspective of race. This is possible not only for reasons I've already stated, but because both positions, regardless of their differences, are minoritarian: each considers itself the minority in the face of the majority's erroneous, dangerous opinions about trans. Despite the supremacy of medical evidence in the legal system, such that medical science is the cornerstone of the determination of rights (Beauchamp 2009: 357), it's likely that some liberal-simplified, defanged version of identitarianism is gaining more traction in the mainstream, given the popularity of the "sex is between your legs, gender is between your ears" soundbyte, among other things. But without "smashing the gender binary," these kinds of concessions to the identitarian framework are seen as gentrification which upholds medicalization's hegemony (indeed, a strong case). This again resonates with terms used in race discourse, pointing again to the racialized nature of Western trans discourse.

Of course, the use of a racializing positionality is not new in queerness, whether it's the minoritarian frameworks mentioned above, the unacknowledged labor of trans women of color in the Stonewall era, gay white men talking like black women, or transfluid white man Jack Halberstam concluding a lecture with a clip from the film Times Square in which three white queer punk women perform a song where they identify themselves with racial and homophobic slurs. Halberstam rues the political correctness of our era, pining for a time when the politics on display in the film were possible. Given his institutional standing, it's worth asking: when exactly did they go away?

Freud said female sexuality is the dark continent of psychology. Ono and Lennon said woman is the nigger of the world (does this mean black women are "double niggers?"). Joe Biden said transgender issues are "the civil rights issue of our time." Gloria Anzaldúa's biggest inspiration for mestizaje was the eugenicist Vasconcelos, who believed race-mixing would eradicate the "inferior Negro" (Sexton 2003) through love (eros), not war. The "human biodiversity" position according to which race (as genetic threshold) determines intelligence is common. People will probably never stop using the rhetorical term "wage slave." The discourse of "passing" in trans is directly lifted from race. I could literally go on and on: race as metaphor and racializing positionalities proliferate endlessly. They serve as platforms for radicalization, erasing the violence they do to black queers and the exclusivist inefficacy of their frameworks for anything other than branding.

The intimate relation between race and surveillance that I traced in the previous section carries over from what Marx might call the economic "superstructure" into cultural discourse and social relations. The regimes of legibility I discussed in the divide regarding the definition of trans are informed by the surveillance of the black body, both in the racialized medical-industrial complex's production of "evidence of trans brains" and in the identitarian focus on performing legible narratives whose pathos derives from appropriated, whitewashed statistics of black trans circumstances. Dictating normative gender and variation from that norm in western society is made possible via capitalism's manichean racial nucleus, which makes blackness multiple in its symbolic capacity but also inhuman—in other words, not a single being.

sidony o'neal, *untitled*, 2016.
Glass, cement, copper, saltwater, pork rind, imitation vanilla.
Dimensions variable. Image courtesy the artist and PNCA Gallery 511.

5.
THE TRANSVALUATION OF TRANS

Just as queerness has been generalized to encompass all norm deviation in nature, trans has been generalized, leaving the realm of gender to describe other neural, social, and economic circumstances. Examples include trans-abled people, trans-species or otherkin people, and trans-racial or -ethnic people. I consider this latter example at length, given this paper's focus on the presence of race in both transgender and generalized "post-trans" discourses. Orthogonal to the generalization of trans is a generalization in trans via the asterisk, whereby the term "trans*" comes to be applied to nonwestern, nonwhite gender deviance and nonconformity in an attempt at symbolic inclusivity that instead imposes identitarian regimes of legibility, mirroring and aiding settler-colonial capitalism as well as subsuming their lived circumstances to bolster the pathological power of the currency of "trans" in the oppression olympics. These two examples make clear that gender is a racial construct, not a universal one: imposition, not inherence.

Transracial or transethnic identity politics lifts the discourse of trans to argue that one was born into the wrong race/ethnicity, and is in reality a member of some other race/ethnicity. Before Rachel Dolezal, the most visible deployments of the term can be seen on tumblr, to varying degrees of performative sincerity. I want to sidestep not only potential responses about what "race really is," since it is very much a legal construct, but I also want to sidestep clearly-perfunctory concerns about whether the trans-racial condition is "real," an instance of internet trolling, an advanced case of racism, transphobia, and cultural appropriation, a symptom of mental disability, or whatever else—since obviously it is or can be all of these—in order to consider what I term here the transvaluation of trans, borrowing a term from Nietzsche.

In his framework, Christianity inverted nature, imposing repression of desires and the elevation of the weak over the strong. He proposed a transvaluation of the Christian west's necrophilic, antipathic moral system in order to return to the violence and virility of the natural order. I want to argue that a similar (and similarly violent) transvaluation occurs in the generalization of trans, both internal and external to the trans community, and that this transvaluation is latent in the manichean racial nucleus of capitalism. This inadvertently aligns "true trans" with a Christian-like position of martyrdom or empire, which I do for the sake of teasing out the hegemonic implications and aspirations of western trans discourse.

Harry Elam argues that blackness is capable of "traveling on its own, separate and distinct from black people... it remains exceedingly attractive in this post-black, postsoul age of black cultural traffic to love black cool and not love black people." (Elam 2005: 386). Orthogonal to this analysis, Hortense Spillers posits that black culture is critical culture as such. If capitalism is fundamentally the attempt to naturalize its generative manichean racial nexus, then the lived experience of blackness is a position of criticality toward this naturalization. Put more simply, if capitalism says "black is this," blackness says "no... yes, even (as drag, as signifying), but also no, never..." But under the regime of epidermalization, where capitalism does say "black is this" and "this is black," with devastating effects, the fluid cool of the idea of the critical position travels past—and gains momentum from—those who actually live and die its consequences. When Biden calls transgender discrimination the "civil rights issue of our time," he is engaging in this long history of muting the critical position to tropeify its power.

The irony of "transracial" discourse is, of course, that race was always already transracial. The 1896 Plessy v. Ferguson decision, which institutionalized Jim Crow segregation, came about as a solution to the problem of white-passing blackness: blackness that could not be seen in the way capitalism's manichean racial nucleus needs it to be. Redolent of Morton's claims about the problem of determining "genuine" code sequences from viral insertion, the "separate but equal" doctrine was meant to prevent the limit case of invisible blackness—a white-passing creole man like Homer Plessy who identified as an "octoroon," that is, seven-eighths white and one-eighth black—from infecting white civil society. In the face of the possibility of this illegible blackness, the solution was quarantining all blacks, setting the stage for modern redlining and data collection policies.

The trope of invisible blackness, from the long history of passing politics to contemporary online "post-trans" discourses such as the transracial, is a condition of possibility for the paradigm of invisible transness. We can see the effects of this paradigm in the racialized imposition of the asterisk in "trans*" when applied to gender-nonconforming people who don't trans-identify, such as people outside the west. The asterisk is a software metaphor, a nod to the wildcard search operator. Here's Google's definition:

> *   Add an asterisk within a search as a placeholder for any unknown or wildcard terms. Use with quotation marks to find variations of that exact phrase or to remember words in the middle of a phrase.
> Example: "a * saved is a * earned"

Essentially, the wildcard operator is a placeholder for which Google's algorithm tries to find the best matches. The idea that the asterisk is "inclusive" is a misunderstanding—all it does is set up a situation where Google "fills in the blanks." As such, the wildcard in "trans*" can only ever symbolically include whatever is

"Googleable," metaphysically speaking—that is to say, legible in the context's given regimes of visibility. Whatever isn't already in the digital corpus will never show up, no matter how many wildcards one uses. This metaphor becomes doubly-ironic given how counterintuitive it would be to explain to the 60% of the world that doesn't have internet access, or the large population of gender-nonconforming people to whom trans has no relevance. Examples like transracial discourse and the politics of the asterisk make clear that gender is a racial construct. The "space" of gender and sexuality, consisting of performativities, identities, orientations, and so forth, is made possible by the racialized logic of visible difference, which has its roots in slavery and its afterlife. Gender deception itself became racialized after 9/11, such as in 2003 when the Department of Homeland Security released an official Advisory warning that "Terrorists will employ novel methods to artfully conceal suicide devices. Male bombers may dress as females in order to discourage scrutiny." The criminalization of "failing" to pass as a woman rests of the assumption that the racialized presentation is a costume, a concealment of some weapon or other nexus of violence – to repeat Chamayou's claim, it is the unknown itself which becomes targeted.

But visible difference, be it dark skin or a racialized regime of gender normativity, is only visible as such because of these kinds of hegemonic assumptions. Transracial identity politics generalizes the spatial metaphor of gender noncomformity to simultaneously posit for the self-evidence of racial identity and the impossibility of locating it. But this paraadox is only a restatement of racism's fundamental premise, because regardless of the use of transracial discourse today, race already was transracial. The politics of the asterisk are a mirror image of transracial discourse, a form of colonialism via arguing that gender is a universal category applicable to all based on racially-informed observations of noncomformity. These two examples make explicit the hegemonic assumptions and implications of western trans discourse itself. But they also serve as the "rock and hard place" between which Black and Brown gender-nonconforming people find themselves: expected to bite our tongues and be grateful for inclusion in pinkwashed, nationalist trans discourses, but also forced to navigate white regimes of legibility to survive.

At its white heart trans is a regime of gender legibility, be it medical evidence or performing identity politics. But, just as with all histories of categorizing and surveilling visible and invisible difference, under the sigil of the signifier we, the damned, accumulate: the transtrenders and post-queers and afronihilists and all the other incalculables of visible difference for whom "trans" is a "best fit," a placeholder for a thing we don't even have the right to name yet. The discarded multiplicity of the Middle Passage traveling epigenetically across generations, the traumatized incalculable flesh that haunts the imago of epidermalization, a fugitive dysaesthesia rejecting all dialectical synthesis of the abject, instead reveling in the carnival. A medical label becomes a coping mechanism becomes a community becomes a politics becomes a metaphysics. The institutions scramble to keep up. It is exactly this indeterminate, inborn generalizability, the way that, as Wittgenstein put it, meaning is use, that allows "trans" to always already transvalue itself. While this open semantic field can lead down paths that, to me, seem questionable or limited in their use—such as transracial identity politics or the symbolic inclusivity politics of the asterisk—we can't but celebrate the most radical political acts of all: Black and Brown people continuing to survive in "this world," and refusing to say "this world" as if it makes sense.

BIBLIOGRAPHY

Banks, Taunya Lovell. 2006. Mestizaje and the Mexican Mestizo Self: No hay Sangre Negra, So There is No Blackness. Southern California Interdisciplinary Law Journal 15.2 (199-234).

Beauchamp, Toby. 2009. Artful Concealment and Strategic Visibility: Transgender Bodies and U.S. State Surveillance After 9/11. Surveillance & Society 6.4 (356-366).

Department of Homeland Security. 2003. DHS advisory to security personnel; no change in threat level. Department of Homeland Security. http://www.dhs.gov/xnews/releases/press_release_0238.shtm.

Department of Homeland Security. 2008. Real ID. Department of Homeland Security. http://www.dhs.gov/xprevprot/programs/gc_1200062053842.shtm.

Elam, Harry. 2005. Change Clothes and Go: A Postscript to Postblackness. Black Cultural Traffic: Crossroads in Global Performance and Popular Culture. Ann Arbor: University of Michigan Press.

James, Joy. 2009. The Dead Zone: Stumbling at the Crossroads of Party Politics, Genocide, and Postracial Racism. South Atlantic Quarterly 108.3 (459-481).

Johnson, Charles R. 1993. The Phenomenology of the Black Body. Michigan Quarterly Review 32.4 (pp 599-614).

Morton, Timothy. Year. Queer Ecology. PMLA 125.2 (273-282).

Muñoz, José Esteban. 2009. Cruising Utopia: the Then and There of Queer Futurity. New York: NYU Press.

Noble, Safiya. 2013. Google Search: Hyper-visibility as a Means of Rendering Black Women and Girls Invisible. InVisible Culture: Issue 19: Blind Spots.

Parenti, Christian. 2004. The Soft Cage: State Surveillance in America from Slavery to the War on Terror. New York: Basic Books.

Raengo, Alessandra. 2013. On the Sleeve of the Visual: Race as Face Value. New Hampshire: Dartmouth College Press.

Rosenberg, Jordana. 2014. The Molecularization of Sexuality: On Some Primitivisms of the Present. Theory & Event 17.2.

Sexton, Jared. 2003. The Consequence of Race Mixture: Racialised Barriers and the Politics of Desire. Social Identities 9.2 (241-275).

Sexton, Jared. 2008. Amalgamation Schemes: Antiblackness and the Critique of Multiracialism. Minneapolis: University of Minnesota Press.

Spade, Dean. 2003. Resisting medicine, re/modeling gender. Berkeley Women's Law Journal 18 (15-37).

Spillers, Hortense J. 2006. The Idea of Black Culture. The New Centennial Review 6.3 (pp. 7-28).

Spillers, Hortense J. 1987. Mama's Baby, Papa's Maybe: An American Grammar Book. Diacritics 17.2 (64-81).

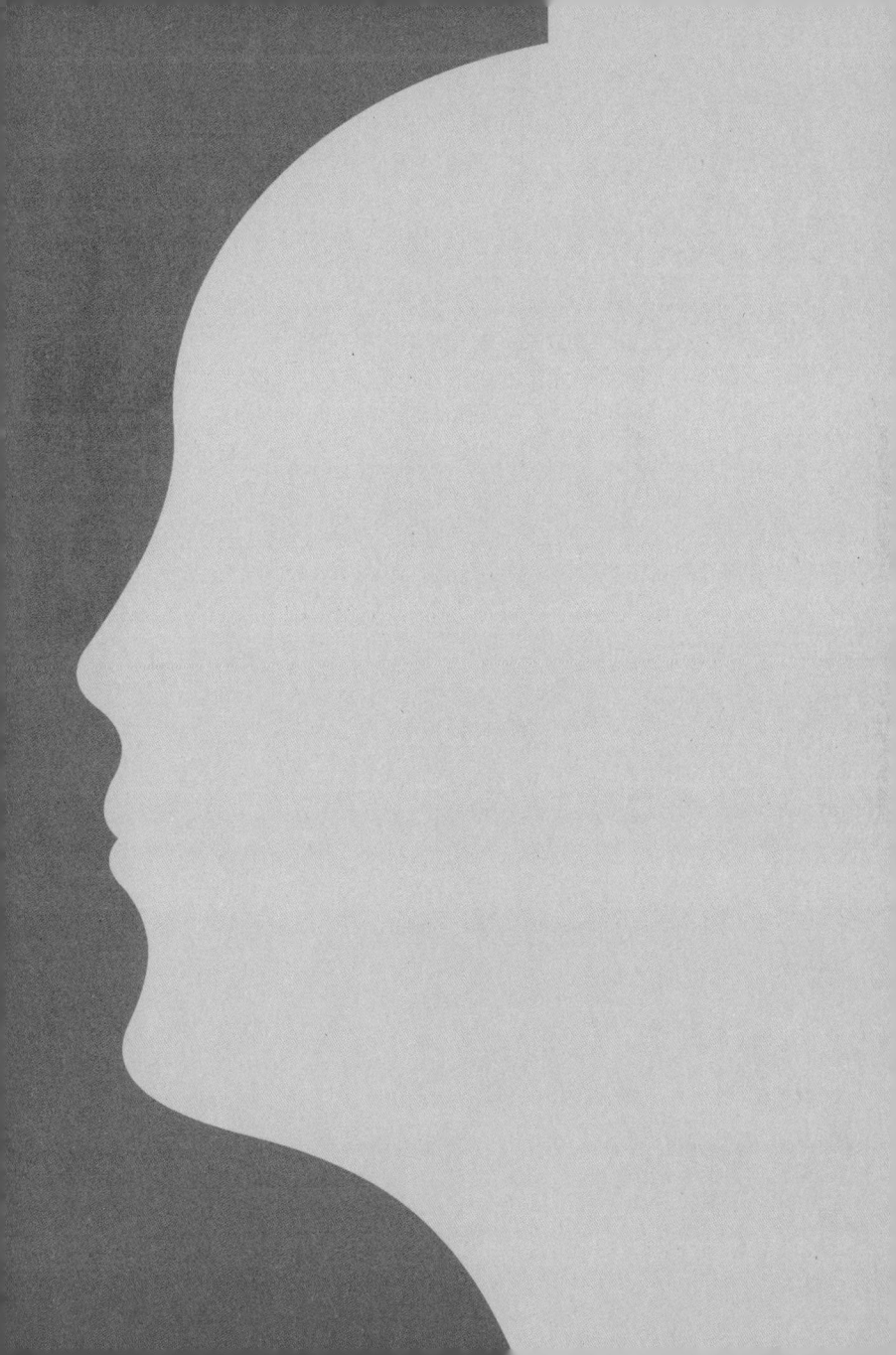

IS
THE FACE
A SCREEN?

"The first word of the face is the "Thou shalt not kill." It is an order. There is a commandment in the appearance of the face, as if a master spoke to me. However, at the same time, the face of the Other is destitute; it is the poor for whom I can do all and to whom I owe all And me, whoever I may be, but as a 'first person,' I am he who finds the resources to respond to the call."

—Emmanuel Levinas[1]

Emmanuel Levinas tells us that the face of the other, in its defenseless nudity, cries out: "Do not kill me."[2] The face "orders and ordains" us, "as if a master spoke" to us, framing an encounter between oneself and one's duties to the other.[3] For Levinas, the other's face "accuses" us with its naked frailty—not with speech but with expression—and for this reason the encounter forms the basis of ethics: its very exposedness or weakness gives it power. Levinas claims that at this site of encounter, the self must decide how to respond to the cry of the face, which punctures the vacuum-sealed world of personal desires and intentions to present itself as *more real*, as the hole of "signification without context," which reveals the possibility of an outside to quotidian reality. "The face speaks," Levinas says, as "it renders possible and begins all discourse."[4] But the speech is not linguistic; on the contrary, the face is a "nonlin-

---

1. Levinas, Emmanuel. 1985. *Ethics and Infinity: Conversations with Philippe Nemo.* Pittsburgh: Duquesne University Press.
2. Levinas, Emmanuel. 1969. *Totality and Infinity.* Boston: Martinus Nijhoff Publishers.
3. Levinas 1985: 97
4. Ibid.

guistic point of reference that also enables us to break the vicious circularity of the symbolic order." This rupture "provides it with the ultimate foundation, the 'absolute authenticity.'"[5]

In developing his position, Levinas broke with his teacher Martin Heidegger and shifted the ground of philosophy from the self and contemplation of the self's mortality (being-toward-death, *Sein-zum-tode*) to the call of the other. In particular this contemplation regarded the *other*'s mortality, embodied in the "defenseless nudity" of the face, which holds unspeakable power over the gazer according to Levinas. In ineffable expressivity it calls out to us, commands us. But a cursory glance at the violence of history and the present calls Levinas' formulation into question. If the face had the kind of power he claimed, then the settler, the slaver, the officer, and the speculator would have been "ordered and ordained" not to kill.

Moreover, if the face is indeed signification without context or meaning before language, then it has significant structural overlap with the hyperreality of commodities, which are empty signifiers unmoored from context, with which we are also in asymmetrical relations. It would be reductive to read Levinas' use of "other" as pointing to "othered" people, but the reductiveness is instructive in light of this overlap: the face of the other may be able to launch wars, but it has not stopped the ongoing march of violence and exploitation. Its thrall over the gazer seems to only go in one direction, toward violence and marketization. According to Slavoj Žižek, anchoring ethics to the other's face as Levinas would have it is therefore "a priori impossible, since the limitation of our capacity to relate to Other's faces is the mark of

---

5. Žižek, Slavoj. 2006. *The Neighbor*. Chicago: University of Chicago Press, 5.

our very finitude."[6] Instead, for Žižek, the face of the other does the work of "cementing normativity."[7]

Encounter with the bottomless other means accepting one's own limitations and mortality. One's own life is framed by the deaths of others, by one's relation to those deaths. To continue the proposed reductive reading of Levinas above, the cry of others' faces is exactly what most Western people spend their lives trying to avoid confronting, hearts full of vague dread with the sense that, in whatever intangible way, we are responsible. For what? For everything, given the violence and wastefulness of so many modes of Western existence. And it is the not-knowing, the impossibility to articulate, that may cause the most pain, because "avoiding the other's face" is ultimately as self-centered and necropolitical as white Western savior complexes are. In this way the West treats the other's face (the "othered" face) as a kind of screen—a surface of mediation.

Žižek argues that "the limitation of our ethical relation of responsibility toward the Other's face [...] necessitates the rise of the Third (the domain of regulations)."[8] The encounter between self and other entails the presence of another, a mediating force like the State which Levinas calls 'the third.' Here we can begin to see the true treatment of the other's face, and the reaction of the Western self to its wordless accusation and gesture toward one's finitude. The other's face is a kind of landscape of colonial shame, a screen the Western self uses to project the presence of the State—the settler, the slaver, the officer, the speculator—and simultaneously deny the existence of anything but the (Western) self.

---

6. Ibid 184
7. Ibid. 5
8. Ibid

Still from L'Arrivée d'un train en gare de La Ciotat (1895).
Image courtesy Association Frères Lumière.

What is this screenlike quality of face of the other? It's redolent of the Lumière effect, named after the legendary story in which the train depicted in the Lumière brothers' 50-second film *L'Arrivée d'un train en gare de La Ciotat* (1895) caused audiences to jump out of their seats and stampede out of the theater in terror, so realistic did the train seem. Film scholar Martin Loiperdinger writes: "Such a tale of more or less drastically amplified panic assumes naïve viewers who had the wool pulled over their eyes and therefore succumbed to a filmic delusion of reality... the affective power ascribed to the medium [of cinema] is postulated to operate suggestively; that is, the medium is supposedly capable of deactivating spectator consciousness, inevitably drawing all under its spell."[9] The notion of mistaking representation for re-

---

9. Loiperdinger, Martin. 2004. Lumiere's *Arrival of the Train:* Cinema's Founding Myth. *The Moving Image* 4.1, Spring, pp. 89-118.

ality resonates with the way that, for the Western self, the face of the other implies and requires the third perspective (such as the State) to mediate, translate, sublimate. And the resulting panic of this conflation allows one to consider how, for the West, the other's face justifies the necessity of the State, as well indicating the West's own always-already mediated, even imaginary status. The other's face demands a suspension of disbelief in the Western mind, for it is like an event horizon in its accusation, revealing nothing regardless of the quality of the gaze.

Time after time, conquest after conquest, the West continues to see reality as secondary to imaginary, timeless, perfect forms, whatever shape these pseudo-concepts take. Confronted with reality's violence, the Western mind turns to skepticism: disbelief un-suspended, theater lights turned back on, snacks eaten. *I'm unsure if anything except me is real.*[10] The other appears as all variety of monsters and fantastical beings, and the West believes all manner of reaction is justified in the terrifying encounter justly described by Levinas. "I've already called the cops"—one takes the role of the State into one's own hands.

And yet, the face of the other is sticky: afterimages remain, haunting the conceptual space that the Westerner thought had been cleared by State intervention. These traces have a Lacanian flair of a Big Other that structures or govern the anxieties and reactionary impulses of the western subject. Thus the other's face takes on the phantasmagoric properties of the commodity,

---

10. The skeptical or solipsistic position – the crown jewel of genocidal Western thought – evidences properties of eternal return, since as Whitehead notes western philosophy is a footnote to Plato (Whitehead, 1979. *Process and Reality*, p. 39)

to cite Benjamin[11]. Its expressiveness is reduced to a platform for self-actualization.[12] Žižek argues that the other's face is the ultimate fetish, inscribing the terms of normativity for the Western mind.[13] The very expressivity, the screen-like quality, of the face, is the means by which the Western subject protects itself from the violence of reality, from the actual terror of that face, which reminds one of complicity in the other's pain.

The need for constant transparency and instant availability is another result of the West's treatment of the other's face as a screen.[14] The state and its machinations are conduits for an on-demand narrative, a fantasy of total transformative access. The saving grace of the terrifying other's face is the potential for translation, for reduction, and for the manufacturing of sellable templates. The other's face is so often treated as a customizable template—even now, as I theorize the face, I am embodying this behavior. The reality of the other is concealed by the inherently-mediated nature of the face and its cry. With its ostensible gestural universality and infinite difference, the prelinguistic accusation of the other is shot back toward the self's gaze. The Western self, who has always already called the State, projects the self's actions onto the face of the other, and sees in the expressions of the other's face the justification for a return to normative vio-

---

11. Cohen, Margaret. "Walter Benjamin's Phantasmagoria." New German Critique 48 (1989): 87-107.
12. Markus, Gyorgy. 2001. Walter Benjamin or: the Commodity as Phantasmagoria. *New German Critique* 83. Duke University Press, 3-42.
13. For Žižek, "the human face 'gentrifies' the terrifying Thing that is the ultimate reality of our neighbour." Žižek, Slavoj. 2004. A Plea for Ethical Violence. The Bible and Critical Theory 1:2. Monash University ePress, 5.
14. Žižek says that "if we stick to the postulate of a final translatability of the Third into

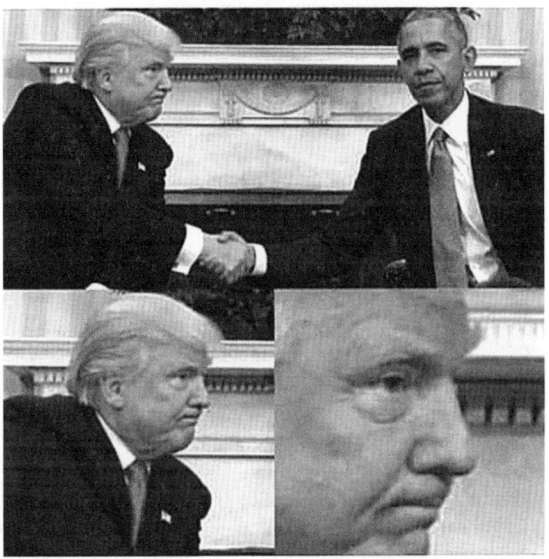

Image courtesy http://me.me.

lence. From this, then, we see the driving force behind contemporary art projects such as Zach Blas' *Facial Weaponization Suite*, the artist and participants made "collective masks" in workshops that are modeled from the aggregated facial data of participants, resulting in amorphous masks that cannot be detected as human faces by biometric facial recognition technologies.

Blas' masks are protective devices fashioned from data from the very systems of surveillance that generate the threat of the other's face. Rather than allowing the military-industrial surveillance complex to flatten reality into its clusters of statistical aggregates, Blas' work weaponizes these panoptic conditions. His masks speak to the constructed nature of the other's face, how its properties are symptoms of a larger system and not essential to that other. Said another way, in the contemporary Western rubric the face of the other is virtual. Representation is mistaken for reality, a mediator is needed to resolve the mistake. The politics of hope in Levinas' claims —the hope that the face is enough to convince us not to kill—mirrors the suspension of disbelief of cinema, and also implies the ostensibly infinite customizability offered to users by the heavily templatic ecosystem of virtuality. Both involve a similar degree of projection premised on the phantasmagoric nature of the commodity, which, unmoored from context, appears as "more real" than the mundane world. The face of the other was like God for Levinas, or a godly trace, but gods in the West have mostly given way to movie stars, to the e-famous, to personal "spirituality." Levinas did not see the ways in which the other's face, as well as the othered face, are forced to play a role in mediation, to act as stand-ins for the State.[15] For him, it was an unmediated surface, whereas in our time, the surface itself is the mediation.

However, Blas' masks are still that: masks, meant for subterfuge. This is ultimately a reactionary gesture, which continues to trap in "a relation to the Other's face," due to which "we remain caught in the vicious cycle of 'understanding,'"[16] since the mask only covers the face, it doesn't offer a new way of looking. We can

---

15. The instances of marginalized people being labeled "PC [political correctness] Police" are evidence of this.
16. Žižek, Slavoj. 2006. *The Neighbor.* Chicago: University of Chicago Press, 184
17. Glissant, Édouard. 1997 [1990]. *Poetics of Relation.* Ann Arbor: University of Michigan Press, 190

look to another framework -- that of opacity -- to challenge the essentialism at play and "perhaps, give up this old obsession with discovering what lies at the bottom of natures."[7] Martiniquan theorist Edouard Glissant argues that instead of projecting fungible conflations of representation and reality onto the face of the other, it is possible to respect its fathomless expression; the unknowability of the face can actually be generative, not terrifying. What Levinas calls an accusation on the part of the other is, to Glissant, in fact the presence of opacity, which forces the self to face its own limitations of knowledge and experience. For Glissant, self and other can exist in relation without the miasmatic screen of projection, the toxic white imaginary, if this opacity is respected — that is to say, not breached, reduced, commodified, or vilified. He writes:

> How can one reconcile the hard line inherent in any politics and the questioning essential to any relation? Only by understanding that it is impossible to reduce anyone, no matter who, to a truth he would not have generated on his own. That is, within the opacity of his time and place. Plato's city is for Plato, Hegel's vision is for Hegel, the griot's town is for the griot. Nothing prohibits our seeing them in confluence, without confusing them in some magma or reducing them to each other. This same opacity is also the force that drives every community: the thing that would bring us together forever and make us permanently distinctive [...] We clamor for the right to opacity for everyone.[18]

---

18. Ibid. 194.

Glissant's opacity is not a masking, and is useful for this reason: the same demands for transparency from Western powers-that-be can be challenged by a faceless, decentralized mass, a network of opacity which does not trade on the commodification of sociality and affect, the micromanagement of human time and contemplation. According to this ideal framework, we could respect each other on the basis of our mutual opacity, accepting the non-intelligibility of each to each. Acknowledging the "unknown unknowns" of the other, in this framework, would be the ultimate sign of respect, and the basis for a network of interactions that are not driven by entitlement to instant access or that require constant translation.

Zach Blas. *Facial Weaponization Suite: Fag Face Mask -
October 20, 2012, Los Angeles, CA.*
Photo by Christopher O'Leary

Others feel that there is no escaping the proliferation of marketized templates and flattened sensible categories. In reality, the quality of being templatic is not inherently bad, and the assimilated nature of tools of resistance doesn't necessarily decrease their impact. In the gaps in the network, silence and noise both give way to a slippage / tension / non-space across the violence of metaphor. The West must come to an understanding of the ways in which its reactions to the other's face are projections so that it can begin weaning itself off the deaths of others and the commercial cycle that always follows the other's death. Giving up the need for instant access is a first step, akin to accepting that we will never know what made Bas Jan Ader cry in *I'm Too Sad to Tell You* (1970-71), or rather, that we always knew—it was the audience itself that made him weep.

INCALCULABLE LOSS

The algorithms that make up Big Data distribute complicity for death across the populations they surveil.

Once upon a time, the virtual represented a domain of free play, a realm separate from the flesh, a "second life." But the corporatization of digital architecture and the advent of Big Data have ended this digital dualism. Now, says former NSA director Michael Hayden, "we kill people based on metadata." Now that digital activity is a basis for state violence, the "virtual" and the "flesh" are no longer separate zones. Through mass surveillance, the virtual makes the flesh vulnerable to death, and the flesh lends its reality to virtual calculations. This link between surveillance, data-mining, and death has birthed a new form of necropower (Achille Mbembe's term to describe the politics of deciding who lives and who dies): algorithmic necropower.

The data-mining procedures used by the NSA and other entities draw their predictive power from their use of incalculable algorithms, enabling them to replace causation with correlation. They rely on numbers, not theories. Using huge datasets culled from the surveillance of online activity, Big Data algorithms can discern or generate correlations that would not be apparent to human perception. They test rules against these correlations: How likely is it that someone who spends an hour on the slots will spend 20 minutes playing blackjack? How likely is it that a college-educated ethnic minority will read the *New Inquiry* if they also read the *Wall Street Journal*? The predictions that emerge from these correlations and rules are context-free, but, when interpreted by people, become the basis for advertising campaigns, urban planning, actionable security decisions, and many other aspects of modern society.

Long before Big Data yoked together calculation and incalculability, Derrida described justice as "a calculation within the incalculable." Because every demand for justice is singular, there is nothing it can fully be compared with: It is incalculable, because no other thing can enumerate its content. In this light, the algorithms used in Big Data appear as a kind of perverse instance of justice. The relationship between Big Data and the incalculable algorithms it hosts is reminiscent of the Derridean relationship between justice (a singular demand) and the law (the rule that singularity is held to). The law proceeds according to rules, but justice cannot be arrived at through the application of a rule: Justice is always singular, and always grounded on its own impossibility. It requires an incalculable calculation that we can perform only when at a loss, unable to speak and calculate. But even an incalculable calculation needs a rule, so we still need the law to guide us to justice, at the limits of what can be calculated.

Both mathematically and juridically speaking, powerful tools for modeling, predicting, and manipulating human reality have emerged from these limits. The history of computation is a prime example of the power of language to quantify and exploit life. If language allows us to articulate possible worlds, then the ability to calculate possible worlds at the scale that algorithms allow changes the human relation to history and futurity. While we "grapple" with the incalculable, our algorithms can articulate worlds beyond our grasp, keeping track of the gray zones between finite states, the places our understanding can't go.

Because of how our intelligence works, human logic has to start from the rule of law, from finite states and binaries, even if what we are seeking is the incalculable justice that exceeds the law. But algorithms, able to contain the incalculable, can start *from the ground* of incalculability. Despite the oppressive uses Big Data is put to, this capacity ironically seems to bring it closer to Derrida's understanding of justice. In reality, managing incalculability becomes the basis for new automated modes of organization and control, in an alchemical process that "distills" history into a usable dataset. What remains of justice, when the incalculable can be made to count?

Algorithmic necropower—the computation of who should live and who should die—operates from the basis of incalculability to discern "non-obvious associations." Still, according to the U.S. Inspector General, "association does not imply a direct causal connection." Instead, it "uncovers, interprets and displays relationships between persons, places, and events." Algorithms escape the laws of cause and effect and operate in a fluid state of exception, encompassing the financial sector, the military-security nexus, and the entertainment industry. Although algorithms seem to allow Big Data to bypass human judgment, in fact a huge amount of labor is required to map associations and interpret the output. The algorithm itself has to be written by a human, and even then, it only spits out data; people still have to decide what the data means. Ordinary language and the "ordinary actions" of post-digital citizens act as a database for algorithmic necropower to manipulate reality and generate threats. Risk levels are rated based on activity patterns that seem anomalous in relation to the norms derived from data.

The *norms*, the data relations, are what determine suspicion of terrorist activity, not causal evidence. The "March 2013 Watchlisting Guidance," a leaked government guidebook for putting individuals on terrorist, no fly, and selectee lists, says, "Although irrefutable evidence or concrete facts are not necessary, to be reasonable, suspicion should be as clear and as fully developed as circumstances permit." The document also has loopholes for cases where officials can't articulate reasonable suspicion: Family relations of known or suspected terrorists, individuals who may be "associates" of terrorists, or individuals with a "possible nexus" to terrorism, may be watchlisted.

Reasonable suspicion is thus a computer-aided human judgment based not on causal evidence (fact), but on *data* correlations, on perceived norm deviation. Everyday behavior becomes a means for the state to detect threats, a measure of risk. This architecture distributes complicity in a new way.

In terms of necropower, Mbembe's concern is "those figures of sovereignty whose central project is... the generalized instrumentalization of human existence and the material destruction of human bodies and populations." Who are these figures of sovereignty, when data appears as sovereign? *Who* kills, in algorithmic necropower? The people who coded the algorithms? The generals, managers, CEOs, or shareholders who ordered them? The companies buying and selling the algorithms? The civilians whose surveilled daily lives constitute the bulk of the data the algorithms analyze? *Our* banal activities are the source from which algorithms automatically generate kill lists made up of nodes that deviate from the cluster of normal activity patterns. Algorithmic necropower defers the act of killing and disperses complicity.

For algorithmic necropower, history is over: the past is not a record of causal relations, but raw material for increasing predictive power. At every turn, with each monitored action, data are made calculable. As "regular users" of language and of the algorithms used to reproduce sociality on the Internet, we fashion ersatz individualities in surveilled spaces geared towards consumption. The primary value of this online activity, from the point of view of security operations, is that it provides the norm for the data set probed by algorithms, testing and manipulating association rules. The activities of "making a self" and deciding what and how to consume are not normally considered "work," but in the amorphous terrain of algorithmic war, stretching over various domains of modern life, affect itself becomes financialized, and biological life—bodies in physical spaces—becomes a surplus value where calculable, and, when incalculable, a contagion.

For data-mining corporations, "life" can be categorized according to this distinction: mineable and unmineable activity. The former serves as the database to mount an attack on the latter, as evidenced by the NSA's increased monitoring of users of the TOR encryption network developed by the U.S. Naval Research Laboratory, as well as of visitors of the *Linux Journal* forum page, which the NSA deemed an "extremist forum." Internet activity signaling that the user is conscious of her privacy sets off surveillance algorithms, which predict whether or not this kind of user is subversively aware of the role of her data in the architecture of war.

What halts the algorithmic state of exception? Derrida may provide an answer: the incalculable traces, the self-effacing cinders of language that point beyond language. Computation itself produces immense quantities of incalculable data that are effectively useless. These incalculable traces clog calculation: While incalculable algorithms are quanta of data that guide computation, incalculable data are simply qualia of data, groundless remainders, taking up server space. They're not useful for intelligence or profit. Take the simple example of a curated Amazon product listing, updated in real time: It would generate so much traffic by scraping the site to get price data every, say, half-millisecond that Amazon would have to operate at a loss to maintain the servers necessary to allow the data hemorrhage of the price-mining process.

History is composed both of things that can be known, and things that can't—mineable (calculable) and unmineable (incalculable) events. The latter category comprises not only things that happened without trace, but also the traces of what never happened. Even incalculable algorithms cannot yet enter into this incalculability of experience, which lives as mourning, or hope, or other relations between past, present and future that escape enumeration. Algorithms enumerate quanta of data, but the qualia of data—subjective experiences of the world—cannot yet be captured by algorithms. Nevertheless, our surveilled responses to *qualia*, our online "self-making," loop back into the quantifiable (mineable) zone, as with Facebook's attempts to monitor emotional states.

Yet there is always an incalculable remainder. In the face of the seeming alchemy of the computational process, forgotten or unlived histories proliferate. This remainder of computation is where justice is to be found, guided both by law and by the incalculable, qualitative data of subjective experience. These qualia are not useful to algorithmic computation and are only intelligible to human eyes. One potential sabotage of algorithmic necropower would be for users to actively produce incalculable data. Facial warping such as in the work of the artist Zach Blas represents an aesthetic gesture toward incalculability. But algorithms are faster than humans, if not more inventive. It would be more efficient, if no less realistic, to wait for the authors of the algorithms to undertake a program of sabotage themselves.

If algorithms make complicity incalculable, it is because those who make the algorithms count on avoiding complicity. The idea that the algorithm itself decides is part of the general ideological offensive surrounding its deployment. The politics and interests of its authors may be incalculable from the standpoint of the person or population who is caught up in the algorithm, but this is precisely what the algorithm is intended to calculate. The remainders, the incalculable, messy qualia of particular human politics and interests are equally its ground, and what it will inevitably proliferate.

Algorithms straddle a gray zone between the privatization of war and the financialization of civilian life, acting as the connective fiber to fuse them in order to subjugate "life to the power of death," as Mbembe says. In algorithmic war, "here" and "there" collapse: Ordinary "civilian" activity is a determinant source for state intelligence. Fused across finance, security, and entertainment, this relentless exercise of necropower might also be called necrocapitalism. Life itself becomes a surplus value. At the same time, the residue of history, of incalculable qualia, produced by attempts to read the future, becomes a contagion that Big Data is still struggling to manage. And the longer it goes on, the expansion of this incalculable contagion shows just how small Big Data really is.

ACKNOWLEDGMENTS

'Notes on the Garage Residency' was originally commissioned by SFMOMA's arts and culture platform Open Space for its "Work on Work" column in September 2016.

'Is Theorizing Cannibalism Ethical?' previously appeared in the Hypocrite Reader issue 39 in April 2014.

The Mongrel essays were originally commissioned by Rhizome to accompany the inclusion of the analyzed works, *BlackLash* (1998) and *Heritage Gold* (1998), in the Rhizome Net Art Anthology in January – February 2017.

'Against the Supremacy of Thought' previously appeared in unbag issue 1, but the author redacted it due to editorial differences. Rhizome re-published it online in January 2018.

'Online Imagined Black English' previously appeared in Arachne webzine issue 01 in November 2015.

'Transtrender' previously appeared on the NewHive blog in April 2016.

The Rhizome artist profile was facilitated by Eleanor Ford and published on Rhizome in May 2016.

'Is the face a screen?' previously appeared on the transmediale online journal in April 2018.

'Incalculable Loss' was originally commissioned by the New Inquiry for issue 31 in August 2014.

HEADER IMAGES – IN ORDER OF APPEARANCE

1. Photo of the garage taken by abreu in 2016.

2. Unknown, 'Cannibals on the Caribbean Island' in Lorenz Fries, Uselegung der Mercarthen oder Carta Marina, Strasbourg: Johannes Grüninger 1525, leaf XVI, Woodcut, handcolouring, 10.5 x 14.4 cm, Archive of Early American Images, The John Carter Brown Library, Brown University.

3. Afro Thunder side-eyes the audience. Promotional image from *Ready 2 Rumble Boxing*. Copyright Midway Games Inc.

4. Screen capture of Heritage Gold 1.0, taken in SheepShaver 2.3.

5. manuel arturo abreu, *Herramienta*, 2016. Tallow candle, soursop juice, aluminum can. Dimensions variable. Image courtesy the artist and AA|LA Gallery.

6. Clip art about language and power. Source unknown.

7. 'Composition #8' by Taylor Ervin, username eviltornray. Still image of a NewHive composition.

8. Photo of a veve to Papa Legba by abreu, 2015.

9. Rubin vase clip art.

10. Vectorized video game graphic. Origin unknown. Image courtesy the New Inquiry.

Institute for New Connotative Action Press
http://incainstitute.org/inca-press

EDITIONS:

Forms of Education: Couldn't Get a Sense of It
2016

Free as in Free...
2016

To Make a Public: Temporary Art Review 2011-2016
2017

manuel arturo abreu: Incalculable Loss
2018

Aeron Bergman and Alejandra Salinas: Telepathy 传心术
2018

COLOPHON

Incalculable Loss
manuel arturo abreu

PUBLISHED BY
Institute for New Connotative Action Press

PRINT
Kerschoffset

ISBN
978-0-9977639-3-5

PRINT RUN
750

PRINTED IN
2018, Zagreb

EDITORS
Alejandra Salinas, Aeron Bergman and Irena Borić

COPY EDIT
Amanda Hurtado

DESIGNER
Rafaela Dražić

Creative Commons Copyright manuel arturo abreu. 2018
Attribution-NonCommercial-ShareAlike 4.0 International

http://www.manuelarturoabr.eu

Image copyrights remain with their creators